Contents

Learning is the process whereby knowledge is created through the transformation of experience. This definition emphasizes several critical aspects of the learning process.... First is the emphasis on the process of adaptation and learning as opposed to content or outcomes. Second is that knowledge is a transformation process, being continuously created and recreated, not an independent entity to be acquired or transmitted. Third, learning transforms experience in both its objective and subjective forms. Finally, to understand learning, we must understand the nature of knowledge, and vice versa.

Kolb D.A. (1984)
Experiential Learning: Experience as the Source of Learning and Development, Prentice Hall, p. 38.

Preface

Teachers have an understandable mistrust of pundits, and especially those who do not take daily part in the rough and tumble of the classroom. This is healthy and proper.

Nonetheless, there are problems. Few classroom teachers get the opportunity to see the work of other teachers elsewhere; and few teachers at the end of an exhausting day have the energy to put their experiences into printable form. Increasingly, local advisers and inspectors are suffering from the same problems of overload. It falls to the academics in the tertiary sector to spread the word of what is going on, to try to pull together the unsorted daily experiences of their colleagues at the chalk face and make sense of them, as they interact with the social, technological and political pressures of our time.

In a mixed and jumbled career, which has seemed to make an odd sort of sense, I have spent three-decades-plus in education, crossing back and forth between librarianship, teaching and research, and trying to learn lessons from all three. I have done my classroom stint with rebellious and unmotivated 15-year-olds; I have suffered with my student teachers as we tried to resolve their difficulties together; I have worked with, and had the privilege of studying the achievements of, many able and innovative teachers whose friendship and acceptance has been greatly valued: and before and in the intervals I ran libraries, taught librarians, and sat on endless working parties and committees with teachers, administrators, educational technologists and computer experts, all trying to find ways of making the teacher's life easier and the pupil's experience richer.

None of this gives me any authority whatever to pontificate, or tell any teacher 'what to do'. But that isn't what this book is about — and indeed I know of very few people in the schools and institutes of education who would have the impertinence to be prescriptive in such a way. Because we see many schools in action, talk with very many practising teachers, and have ready access to the books and journals, we act as the middle-men, the communicators, passing on what other teachers are attempting and worrying about and grappling with to those who most need to know, the people in the schools and in the sevices that help them.

Vox et praeteria nihil — I am a voice only, a bringer of messages, a medium for information transmission, seasoned with a modest portion of thought. In the heady days of the Schools Council Resource Centre Project, excited teachers welcomed news of what was going on. This book is written in the hope that it may bring stimulation in equally heady, if much more hectic circumstances.

My thanks to all the people who have knowingly or unwittingly helped. An early version of chapter 1 appeared in the *Education Libraries Bulletin*, whose readers have also shared glimpses of some incidental explorations which here get only a brief report, though they helped me over a hurdle. Particular thanks to the University of London Institute of Education, whose conditions of service allowed me to take a few brief weeks of study leave to get at least the core of this text on to disc and into paper printout. My wife, as ever, helped me through the bad moments and made everything possible. No-one but me, however, should be blamed for the result.

Norman Beswick
November 1986

Chapter 1

Information Systems and Education: The Context of Concern

The future is not what it used to be. The pace of change is hotting up in ways few of us wholly predicted. Economic constraints are worse than we feared: social pressures more insistent: 'revolutions' come fast on each others' tails, each demanding an expenditure of time none of us have left. Many teachers now admit to an almost inevitable pessimism. We know so little: we control so little: we are asked to do so much. Schools cannot themselves resolve the major tensions and blemishes of our world, whatever politicians may sometimes imply at national conferences. The most we can say is that schools have the opportunity of working with and upon children at a time of major importance to them and to us: when they are ready but vulnerable, receptive but easily misled, and when so much that will happen to their learning and motivation remains as mysterious and unpredictable as ever. The world they will inherit does not yet exist, and we know even less about that world than we know about them; yet, as the Faure Report reminded us, it is for that not-yet-existent world that their education must be shaped. We shall as always accommodate, adapt, exploit and improve, but financial cuts are not our only problem, or even our worst one. We shall have to take decisions about our pupils and their future needs before we have enough evidence for more than informed guesses, either on what those needs might be or how best to meet them: indeed, some would argue, before we have absorbed the implications of society, or even our own educational practice, yesterday and today.

The New World of Information Technology

These pages arise from unease about such implications in just one area: the role and use of information materials and technologies. The very

remarkable developments in communications and information technology (including video, the microcomputer, teletext and everything
subsumed under the generic jargon word 'telematics') have made it
fashionable for social commentators and educational pundits to assert,
with evident likeliness, that 'we are entering a new information age'.
Huge quantities of manipulable data will be available to us, to our
students, and to everyone else, at the press of a button, and if other
skills and activities are necessary they are not emphasized by the
advertisers. The result has been a spate of apocalyptic predictions
about the effects of information technology on society in general and
schools in particular.

In itself, this is nothing new. Throughout the past 150 years there
has been increasing futurological speculation of this kind, and it is
always possible that some of the more evidently foolish may yet turn
out to have some truth in them. But let us take a modest and
reasonably responsible example; sociologist Arthur Shostak told
readers of the American educational journal, *Phi Delta Kappan*:

> We may school anywhere (home, office, plant), any time (am
> or pm), in two-way dialogue (instantly or via time-delayed
> sequences), drawing on incredible back-up resources (the
> contents of the world's libraries, museums, organization files)
> and with any one ('superstar' teachers, students of any age or
> geographic locale). The synergistic linkage of communications
> and computer capabilities makes possible bookless libraries,
> paperless news (teletext) and campusless and professorless
> universities — among myriad other mind bogglers.[1]

Shostak is surely right, and is not alone, in thinking that with such a
prospect we had better prepare ourselves. If one thing is at all certain,
it is that the future will in many ways be strikingly different from any
past. The problem however is that it could also be very different from
most prophecies. The snag with prophesying from an evident trend is
that one has to ask, not only 'Where will this lead?' but also 'What else
will be happening at the same time to confuse the issue?'.

In education it is poignant to reflect that down successive decades,
in different terminology and with different technologies, we have
heard a very wide range of claims and a plethora of promises. Even
school libraries, since at least the 1880s and the Cross Commission,
have been set repeatedly to transform education, and every few years
someone has claimed that they must transform themselves into multi-
media centres. Film, said Edison in 1913, would 'completely replace the book in New York schools by the end of this decade'. From

the 1920s onwards, the audio-visual movement was 'certain' to make a huge impact. B.F. Skinner called us all to a marvellous future of programmed learning, asserting that the job was simple, the task could be stated in concrete terms, the necessary techniques were known, and only cultural inertia stood in the way. Closed circuit television came, and went, to be replaced by video. A brand new discipline of 'educational technology' was announced, many of whose prophets are now elaborately distancing themselves from the over-rigorous 'systems approach' they originally propounded. Now we are busily (and very properly) spending our money on microcomputers.

Very little of this was entirely foolish and much had a positive value. There are more examples I could have cited, and most have left their mark in a modest way, yet the revolutions were rarely what they seemed and their effects were less dramatic than the prophets believed. What happens (and most of us have seen this too often for comfort) is a temporary distortion in the pattern of educational life, followed by a reassertion of traditional patterns and traditional structure, mildly amended. The once revolutionary factor becomes a supplementary addition to conventional teaching, used for variety, or when discipline breaks down, or even (it is cynically whispered) when the Deputy Head is eager for promotion.

Remembering this background, it is possible even for the most positive spirit to wonder with a sinking of the heart whether the new information technology will also be absorbed by the omnivorous conservatism of the educational machine. Anyone who has, as I have, spent three decades or more following with enthusiasm the claims of new educational movements, can be forgiven for saying, sadly, 'I have seen the future — and it didn't happen'.

The Perils of Overstatement

What did happen is not necessarily discouraging. Sensible change has been absorbed and teachers spend hours planning for variety, impact, relevance and participation. But why did the multiple revolutions of recent decades fail to make the impact that was predicted? One answer surely is tunnel vision: they were looked at in isolation. Take a comparative analogy from the history of human speed. For most of its span, our species was able to travel at about a maximum of three or four miles an hour, except for very short bursts; we harnessed the horse, and perhaps increased our speed potential five-fold; we invented the steam engine and quadrupled the speed of the horse; the internal combustion engine and the jet engine took us through the sound barrier, and the space rocket opened up even more impressive speeds. So: human beings are now travelling at tens of thousands of miles an hour? Actually no: most of us travel quite a lot on foot, or by bike, and many of us are now being instructed by our doctors to do so more often. We don't all travel at supersonic speeds just because we sometimes can, nor would it be sensible to try. The parallels are obvious.

The exciting thing about the new information technology is that it may nonetheless force us to look at teachers, learners, and resources for learners, with fresh eyes. It really could be a breakthrough this time — but only if we keep our attention on the broader considerations and retain as even a balance as possible between scepticism and optimism. To say that futurology is an exceedingly inexact science does not mean that predictions can comfortably be ignored. The future won't go away, and will certainly bring agonizing difficulties and decisions as well as opportunities. Nonetheless, to say that something is possible is not at all the same thing as saying it is compulsory, or that it is the only possibility, or that unforeseen things will not arise to alter it. The young go-ahead media specialist in the USA in the 1930s stocked up with piano rolls, Victrola records and stereopticons: and whatever happened to quadraphonic sound?

Perhaps more important still, to say that something is possible does not mean either that it is what we want to happen, or that it is the answer we need to have. Jennifer Slack pointed out that the notion of the information revolution 'relies heavily on the acceptance of the notion of autonomous technology'.[2] There are, as she showed, hidden ideological assumptions behind many of the more spectacular prophecies, and it is all too easy to assume without questioning 'the largely unchallenged assumption that increasing technological sophistication automatically produces something called progress, in human terms'. Joseph Weizenbaum, himself a heavy user of computers and the inventor of the famous ELIZA program which mimics the non-directive questioning of one school of modern psychiatry, has passsionately warned us against what he sees as misuses of computer technology[3]; and there is no reputable futurological model which necessarily predicts that human beings will not take note of such warnings and be selective in their use of possibilities.

Returning now to Shostak's prophecy, we can note that to have 'the content of the world's libraries' on immediate call is no universal panacea, even if so enormous an undertaking was felt worth the time and expense. At present we have electronic access to indexes and catalogues only, not the books and journals themselves, whatever may be the future of the electronic journal. Few people seem likely to prefer reading (say) a difficult sociological text on a VDU screen to reading it in an old-fashioned codex book, and technology will have to improve remarkably before an instant print-out on the domestic printer is an acceptable compromise. Rather obviously, a learner who finds one book a problem will not find many millions of books any easier. 'Ah', say the enthusiasts, 'but computers give us the technology to provide access to multiple learning sequences, geared to individual need, through which learners could progress at their own pace'. But alas, technical possibility is not the same as having solved the problem, and there is a growing conviction[4] that we lack the educational and psychological know-how to anticipate all possible responses, and in particular to set a machine to cope with those of a lateral and creative thinker. Moreover, computer technology itself cannot give us the individuals with expertise, backing, foresight and insight to produce learning sequences in the quantity and variety needed. We certainly never managed to develop anything approaching that in the 500 years of that other individualized learning device, the printed book. Computer monitored sequences may not always be the best way for learning difficulties to be tackled, and learners may not always choose, or be able, to use them. Too heavy a reliance on a technology which emphasizes sequential learning, instrumental thinking, and an educational method based on the finding of answers known to exist, rather than sought and created, may well lead to a lop-sided emphasis in our system.

Meanwhile the problems faced by slow learners, new learners, insecure learners and teachers, when faced with vast numbers of learning sequences, multi-megabyte capacity, and the contents of the world's libraries, are not simply daunting: they are horrific. Even a modest book library presents problems of selection and choice, and many readers need help and reassurance. The larger the choice, in these days of the knowledge explosion, the more difficult it is for enquirers to know, not only that they have found the information they want but whether it is still current. Prestel accepts no responsibility for the contents or accuracy of its own files, and perhaps that is too much to expect of huge systems. Libraries, after all, make no such claims — though they usually have skilled staff to offer guidance if requested.

Teachers will try to adapt intelligently to change and make creative use of the new possibilities. Nonetheless teachers in general have been cautious indeed about the kind of learning that comes from secondary sources (we shall discuss 'mere book learning' in the next chapter) and may possibly have, or develop, similar reservations about learning from screens — especially if other people have designed what is on them[5] — and only a salesman would dare to suggest that such caution was necessarily misplaced. We have had five centuries to absorb and develop uses for the printed book; other authors have examined the results in some detail and they give no confidence that we are good at making quick assessments of new learning resources or that it is reasonable to require busy practitioners to do so, faced as they now are with problems of selecting textbooks, library books, av media and now programs. Meanwhile will the technology be standing still? It is much more likely that the pace of change will bring further revolutions to catch our attention, making the microchip and videotex old hat before we have worked out how best to use them. The future will continue to be not what it is.

Far from being destructive, these criticisms point to genuine concern. Undoubtedly our tomorrow will have readily available to it a heavy saturation of information systems old and new, though what is available through those systems will depend on the state of human society as it then is. Let us now make one single addition to the picture: let us place in that 'new information world' a typical young learner of average or below-average achievement (never mind why that level of achievement is what it is — we don't know the answer anyway). It is here that qualms surely crowd quicker and faster. Will a 12-year-old who has difficulty reading a worksheet (in today's terms) find less difficulty in reading a visual display unit? Will someone who has difficulty using the index to a simple book be better able to use the thesaurus of a databank or find a way through Prestel? The problems will surely not be very different. Pressing the button is the least of them. One needs to know which buttons to press and in what order, using what terminology and having made an initial range of conceptual decisions, some of them at quite an advanced level of difficulty. Having found the page or screen of (for instance) text, there is still the problem of decoding or finding meaning in a written and/or verbal account, determining the different kinds and levels of meaning in different kinds of record (some of which may use language in a way that is very different from that which the young learner habitually uses at home) and re-synthesizing them into one's own meaning. Graphics, visuals, statistical tables and the rest increase the complication. The technology brings us more to have to understand.

So far as we can tell, it is not a lack of technology that accounts for the continued existence of students of average and less than average achievement. We lack instead an acceptable explanation of why those levels of learning are as low as they are, and what we could or should be doing about them. It is understanding we lack: technology is secondary.

A disturbing proportion of children (in other countries' schools as well as our own) pass right through the system without achieving functional literacy, and many more emerge from schooling with only a limited competence in reading, writing, numeracy and data seeking. The flexibility of future technology offers creative possibilities for skilled teachers and for learners in search, but this must not lead us to underestimate the continued need for a sound basis of learning theory to underpin it. Frank Smith spoke for many when he wrote in 1978:

> A burgeoning education industry tries more and more to persuade schools to rely on technology rather than understanding in order to teach reading.

Noting that there were 'contemptuous attempts' to produce 'teacher-proof' materials, he continued:

> . . . sophisticated electronic gadgetry is often paired with naive ideas about how learning takes place and about the subject being taught.[6]

This has also been so in other subject areas, and one is relieved to see that some previous, dismayingly simplistic models of machine learning are becoming less evident. Much programming of the 1970s would now be assigned to the 'paleo-' period. Nonetheless, looking at the use of more conventional learning resources and information materials, (such as books and video) it is clear that many teachers lack a secure understanding of their creative deployment. We must grope towards a more thoroughly coordinated understanding of how to exploit recorded information as a teaching and learning tool, and it may be that the new technology will help us to find it, if we can avoid 'tunnel vision'. But this is a hope, not a certainty. There is no inevitable dialectic moving us towards an ultimate illumination.

Thus, when we consider the challenge of the new information technology, and its likely effects on the practice of teachers and the habits and ways of thought of learners (as we hope to do in subsequent chapters) we do well to feel excitement: the prospects are exciting: but we must measure our enthusiastic modernism with a modest caution.

Social Factors and the Diseducated

The problem for educators is compounded, as always, by social disparities. Shostak himself notes how what he calls the community of the haves is relatively quick:

> to profit from the use of home computers, information banks, home video recorders, and other expensive aids, whilst have-nots glare enviously from the sidelines. Lacking the requisite dollars and bereft as well of literacy and numeracy background, have-nots become systematically and progressively more superfluous than before.[7]

This is no novelty: good readers have developed in precisely the same way, as Margaret Clark's influential study[8] made clear. It is commonplace to point out how most children today display greater audio-visual competence than most adult teachers, and young children given the right initial experiences rapidly take to the new information technology in a way that puts the rest of us to shame. Yet, low income families, though not necessarily slow to invest as well as they can afford in new electronic entertainment sources, may be much less enthusiastic about paying for videotex. 'Access to hundreds of thousands of pages of data' may go down well with the prosperous parent who used to buy expensive encyclopaedias to enable the children to 'get ahead', but to the unemployed and disadvantaged it may sound as irrelevant to their needs as the purchase of a quality newspaper. So just as it is the lack of familiarity with books and reading that today drives some teachers to compensatory library-based projects and the vigorous promotion of school bookshops, so it may also be the lack of familiarity with electronic information tools (other than as computer games) that pressurizes teachers to emphasize them in the classroom.

Employers will need some employees with computer competence and information-seeking skills, but many more jobs will be relatively simple tasks prompted by the computer and requiring no great insight into its working. Moreover, we simply do not know at present what proportion of the population will ever be employed. We cannot tell for sure which of our students will fall into which category, and it would be unacceptable to try to distinguish in order to shape their schooling to their future, but questions of motivation inevitably arise. A great many youngsters leave our schools today only partly literate, wholly unable to find their way through the complexity of regulations and opportunities that surround them, but if 'information skills across the curriculum' has the same track record as its distinguished predecessors, this illiteracy is likely to extend into the field of IT. In a society becoming increasingly divisive, piecemeal and uneven development seems appallingly inevitable, with students differently prepared or motivated by their home and social class background, at least in the short to medium term. Yet if we are not ourselves taking the lead, we are likely to be pushed by others into developments dictated by political or other motives, rather than by educational desirability. We have seen this happen many times and the result is inevitably to waste money and temporarily unbalance the curriculum. Parents who know what they want pressure schools for preferential treatment, and raise the money additionally through the parents' association. Meanwhile advertisers and technologists offer us answers. But 'what are the questions?'. Again we ask about the 'use of knowing'.

Only the very complacent would be satisfied with the results of our education system so far. Adult illiteracy in most developed countries is shockingly high, but this is only a symptom of the wider problem. Large numbers of youngsters, especially from disadvantaged backgrounds, leave school not only uneducated but diseducated, 'switched off', hostile to the values education represents and to the skills demanded by a high technology society. Undoubtedly these problems are not helped by governments which deliberately create unemployment as their cure for inflation, and who cut public expenditure on education and the social services in order to be able to reduce taxation for the most wealthy. A sense of community and worth is not encouraged by policies of deliberate confrontation. Teachers may well feel that comprehensive schooling and mixed-ability teaching could hardly have come at a more difficult time, but at least they counter negative factors with a positive statement of intent.

Such alienation has led some concerned educators, and especially those who include the Third World in their span of attention, to ask radical questions about educational systems themselves. Ivan Illich and the deschoolers, who attack the very establishment of schooling, remain influentially on reading lists, and to some teachers the latest technological possibilities linked to a deschooling approach have suggested an opportunity to scrap the present system and go forward on a tack based upon access to information — Prestel online, CAL programs off the shelf, informal networks of help. For Illich, access to information was an important right and the educational establishment was in conspiracy to deny it. Many teachers will have vibrated sympathetically to his declaration that if a person is to grow up, he or she needs 'to see, to touch, to tinker with, to grasp whatever there is in a meaningful setting' (and indeed many will have thought this was what they were trying to do as teachers). This access, Illich said, was denied because knowledge has been made a commodity, and thus potentially private property. His demands were radical-sounding, and he was dismissive about the role of professional teachers:

> there are few mechanical skills used in industry or research that are as demanding, complex and dangerous as driving a car, a skill most people quickly acquire from a peer.[9]

Thus Illich's interest is in the development of 'learning webs', networks of information providers and specialists from whom free learners could gather what they needed in the pursuit of personal quests.

A decade or so later, in the 'new information age', such networks for free learners are in a sense upon us, and we must ask ourselves how far Illich's romantic account justifies our abandoning learners to their use. (We may also ask whether some learners will be voting with their feet.) We learnt the rudiments of our first language without pedagogic help, and most of us can point to learning experiences that happened in spite of schooling rather than because of it. Yet there was no explanation in Illich of how the 'interested learner' was to arise, how that interest was to be maintained through setbacks and discouragements (which may happen because the 'interested learner' has chosen an unhelpful way of learning), and what happened if the interest never came of its own accord — should we just not care? In his distrust of teachers and authority figures, Illich made no allowance for the value of experienced guidance. The deschooled young learner would seem to be more at risk than ever, at the mercy of a random variety of publishers and individuals, who owe no collective loyalty and (crucially) accept no overall responsibility.

Unachieving learners are not greatly helped, and are sometimes created, by the school systems we have, and we must try to make them better. Part of this task is to pay closer attention to the interests, aspiration and world views students bring with them, even if they do not fit easily into the conventional framework. Sometimes it may be advantageous if the individual has access to, and actually uses, an outside information source — whether it be Prestel or the public library; no sensible teacher would resent this. But the unachieving deschooled learner has no means of understanding the range of possibilities opened through knowing, nor of grasping the relevance of learning, 'the use of knowing'. By the time life teaches the lesson (if it ever does) it may be too late.

Thus, schools and teachers remain important as the main guides to entry to the world of information, though they may need more guidance from specialists to help them with the complexities of their mediating role. Deschoolers have been useful in clearing away redundant mythology, even though they have attempted to import further confusion of legend in its place. Yet it is worth noting that deschoolers paid little attention to the enormous growth of interest in teaching methodologies one would have thought very sympathetic to them. It is indeed odd that Illich's fiercest denunciations of educators as authority figures came at a time when curriculum developers worldwide were examining very different attitudes to teaching from those described: in particular, the seemingly progressivist view that education is in some way 'enabling to discover'. It is precisely in this area that old and new information technologies come together, and where the new technology can add an important and perhaps redeeming dimension. Equally oddly, some of the prophets of a new computer-administered education missed it too.

Learning as Enquiry

For Illich and his disciples, the professional teacher was an insensitive controller, dispensing small units of knowledge in a way that maintained teachers' own status and responsibility. Of course we have all met such teachers: they have them in other schools. Computer-assisted learning packages would seem to mimic such teachers, presenting equally small units and sugaring the pill with Olympian comments, such as 'Well done, Johnny'. Yet teachers writing about their work frequently describe themselves quite differently, as 'facilitators of learning' (the terminology varies), their speciality being individual counselling rather than knowledge specialism or mastery of exposition. A Council for Educational Technology statement as long ago as 1970 declared that the teacher's expertise lay:

> in the devizing and organizing of the learning process, in relating it to the needs of particular children, in giving help and support when, and only when, it is necessary....[10]

The document hoped that the second and current industrial revolution might well enable teachers to divert their attention to the organization of learning in terms of the individual child. Such hopes have long been the dream of 'educational technology'; and many teachers have gone on to couple individualization with encouraging the active participation of the student.'Activity' methods long established at primary level (for obvious developmental reasons) were reexamined and adapted for learning in the secondary school. Teachers engaged in 'facilitating learning' saw such methods as crucial to this organization, ranging from the tight control of the unimaginative worksheet to the open-endedness of much 'project', 'enquiry' and 'discovery' learning. Most deschoolers underestimate or ignore this readiness of teachers to think of moving away from instruction to facilitation: a movement that has recently been paralleled by a shift from behavioural to cognitive psychology.

Jerome Bruner has perhaps been the most influential as well as the most sensitive explorer of this approach, and many who initially vibrated in sympathy with the Illich quotation above may nonetheless find much to applaud in the following:

> the hypothesis that I would propose here is that to the degree that one is able to approach learning as a task of discovering something rather than learning about it, to that degree there will be a tendency for the child to carry out his learning activities with the autonomy of self reward or, more properly, by reward that is discovery itself.[11]

Many efforts have been made to put this approach into effect; and it needs to be said that the results have sometimes been disappointing, just as the results intended to validate the theory have also been disappointing. It is one thing to make heart-warming statements about what education should be doing; it is quite another thing to find out how this should be put into effect with 3B on a wet Tuesday. But let it be emphasized that there is no suggestion in Bruner (as there appears to be in the deschoolers and those who prophesy an independent computer-network future) that the learner should be 'abandoned to discovery' without the caring preparation and guidance of the teacher. Whatever else teachers may lack, they have some general idea of what it might be worthwhile and indeed possible to 'discover', and they can provide the stimuli and circumstances leading to meaningful achievement without unnecessary frustration. (They will also benefit from the expertise of specialists.)

Some writers are led by this to speak in terms of a 'process' model of learning rather than a 'content' one. Whether it is necessary to take sides in this is doubtful; students cannot learn the one without the other. But as Dearden[12] commented, discovery methods 'turn on the particular conception of how one is supposed to discover' and not all approaches are either helpful or motivating. Exercises in lab or library clutching a smudgy worksheet, or following a CAL program, are necessarily less exciting, but also less demanding, than combining real world experience plus information found in books and then transforming both by an innovative exercise worked out on the computer. But how can teachers plan the latter and be sure it works — given the lack of planning time and the apparent lack of proven expertise in such methods?

'Learners by discovery' lacking guidance in methodology waste vast amounts of time to no good purpose, and need great good fortune as well as persistent determination to gain any benefit. One of Sartre's novels included a character known as the Auto-Didact, educating himself in a library, where he proceeded alphabetically through a broad-subject catalogue, presumably learning algebra before arithmetic, calculus before trigonometry, the bronze age before the stone age, and Kant before Plato. It might work, but few teachers would plan it that way. The process of discovery cannot be left to hazard, but must develop through a rationale. Teachers and learners will want to explore ways in which the latter are guided towards increasingly active participation in planning their learning, while remaining part of a class or group and contributing to it. The multiplication of facilities for identifying, locating and manipulating information will obviously be helpful, though there will be a great deal to understand and plan (see chapter 3).

The detail of what is involved is lost in the dust cloud arising from the quarrels between factions. Most teachers would claim to be interested in developing the transition from (as it were) 'teaching' to 'learning'; but they need reassurance. A great deal of activity is seen in schools, but where it is not just 'busy work' keeping youthful energies occupied and constraining trouble-makers, it tends still to resemble (and in essence to be) another form of directed teaching. Teachers who wish to move on from this find much of the theory unproven and the essential bases of good practice unresolved.

This fairly obvious point needed to be made (despite the friendly interest these pages will show in enquiry learning) because it would be easy to deduce from much of the literature of education in recent decades that a great deal of autonomous learning was taking place in practice in our schools. Idealistic students write enthusiastic essays to this effect. The Schools Council General Studies Project provided a variety of resource packages which it was hoped would offer the means by which autonomous study could occur. Roberts investigated how the materials were in fact used and found that teachers (despite the intentions of the GSP designers) used the resources predominantly as 'teaching aids' for themselves. Not only did they then criticize their design, but also they showed no sympathy with (and unawareness of the possibility of) the Project's purpose. Meighan and Roberts, commenting on the study, found:

> in the schools studied, the transmission ideology of education, with its particular theories of knowledge, learning, relation-ships, assessment etc, appears to be dominant.[13]

In many ways these conclusions are not surprising to anyone who has looked at the use of any kind of information material, purpose-packaged or not, in the average school, or who has sought a clearly articulated theory for their deployment. We shall examine impli-cations in other chapters, and particularly in chapter 3. Meighan and Roberts found their results 'disturbing' and thought the GSP was 'possibly ahead of its time'. That is a way of putting it. In their own words, what we have at present is a 'teaching-based system which provides some opportunities for independent learning', a judgment many would accept. Their preferred alternative, 'an independent learning system which provides opportunities for teaching', shifts the balance decisively in ways which are becoming more possible, and which need careful and friendly examination, but about which most teachers will need considerable explanation as well as support.

The arrival of 'the new technology' may well make these and other possibilities easier to achieve: but by itself, technology is simply technology. If we want it to be used for specific educational purposes, it is for us to decide how and why, work out the strategies and take over the challenge — if the future allows. But it cannot yet be said that we have gathered from experience a strong theoretical base to do so, and this might be (as we shall try to show) worth attempting.

Many early uses of computer information technology were narrowly instructional, based heavily on programmed learning, and well deserving Oettinger's famous description of using the machines as 'expensive page turners'.[14] Of course, when trying out new technology, it makes sense to begin with simpler operations and build outward, especially as programming a computer calls for much the same linear and logical analysis as devizing a programmed book. All inventions tend first to be used for old-fashioned purposes until their other, newer functions become apparent. We don't dismiss the spirit duplicator because some people use it to produce illegible worksheets, nor the blackboard or overhead projector because some teachers use them for dull notes for lengthy class copying, 'in silence please'.

Fortunately there is plenty of creative potential which one hopes will be readily exploited, and signs of welcome interest from some teachers. The microcomputer can be used for learning games, simulations, extrapolations and creative writing; they can develop aesthetic effects as well as mathematical formulae; and they will be excellent tools for acquiring and practising the skills of information handling and research, including the reworking of what is found into new knowledge. With so wide a range of uses to exploit, no-one should complain if the micro is also used for simple drill; drill can be helpful. Our challenge is to use the facilities of the microcomputer, of videotex and other good things (such as the interactive videodisc just becoming available) in ways that justify the expense and the potential, and make learning more interesting and stimulating than before. The financial implications will be examined in our final chapter; meanwhile we shall try to avoid 'tunnel vision' and explore other implications in a wider context. This means looking at purposes, and how (or whether) the arrival of new technology alters our perception of what those purposes should now be. We shall concentrate as far as we can on the active learner, rather than accidents of format, and (which will seem strange to some) enquiring into uses of the older technology to see if they can inform and improve our strategies for the new.

Seven Conclusions So Far

1   We may expect a dramatic increase in the number of routes to recorded knowledge openly available to us.
2   We may expect an exciting increase in our ability to manipulate bits of that knowledge in new extrapolations, using the new technology.
3   We can only guess at the best uses of these facilities and their effects on our lives, but there is little to suggest that they will remove what have always been major problems for education.
4   We shall have access to more machines, and more cheaply (the reader impressed by today's economic plight, or doctrinally in favour of cutting public spending forever, need not stop reading) but we are not machines ourselves and shall still be making human decisions on their use.
5   What we know about learning theory is less secure than we would

like, but it is not suddenly invalidated by the coming of the microchip.

6 The people who will have the chance to use the new facilities will closely resemble the people who could have made more use of earlier information sources from papyrus onwards, and were often inefficient or confused about it.

7 There will in future be more ways still of knowing, but we must remain concerned with what follows: the interrogation and manipulation and interiorisation of knowing — with 'the use of knowing'.

Notes

1. SHOSTAK, A.B. (1981) 'The coming systems break: Technology and schools of the future', *Phi Delta Kappan* 62, 5, January, pp. 356–9.
2. SLACK, J.D. (1984) 'The information revolution as ideology', *Media, Culture and Society* 6, pp. 247–56.
3. WEIZENBAUM, J. (1976) *Computer Power and Human Reason: From Judgement to Calculation.* San Francisco, CA, Freeman.
4. See, for instance COLLIS, B. (1984) 'Implications of the educational use of computers in North American elementary schools', *British Journal of Educational Studies*, XXXII, 2, June, pp. 125–33; DAVID, P. (1983) 'Should there really be an Apple for the teacher?', *Times Educational Supplement*, 11 November, p. 13; McCANN, P.H. (1981) 'Learning strategies and computer-based instruction', *Computers and Education*, 5, pp. 133–40; SUHOR, C. (1983) 'Cars, computers and curriculum', *Educational Leadership*, 41, 1, September pp. 30–2.
5. STEVENS, D.J. (1980) 'Why computers in education may fail', *Education*, [California] 104, 4, summer, pp. 370–6.
6. SMITH, F. (1973) *Psycholinguistics and Reading.* New York and London, Holt, Rinehart and Winston.
7. SHOSTAK, A.B. (1981) *op. cit.*, p. 358.
8. CLARK, M. (1976) *Young Fluent Readers: What Can They Teach Us?*, London, Heinemann Educational Books.
9. ILLICH, I. (1971) 'The alternative to schooling', *Saturday Review of Education*, June, reprinted in Fantini, M.D. (Ed.) (1976) *Alternative Education: A Course Book for Parents, Teachers, Students and Administrators*, New York, Anchor Books, pp. 34–48.
10. TAYLOR, G. (Ed.) (1970) *The Teacher as Manager: A Symposium*, London, Councils and Education Press for NCET.
11. BRUNER, J. (1974) *Beyond the Information Given: Studies in the Psychology of Knowing*, London, Allen and Unwin, p. 406.
12. DEARDEN, R.F. (1967) 'Instruction and learning by discovery', in PETERS, R.S. (Ed.) *The Concept of Education*, London, Routledge and Kegan Paul.
13. MEIGHAN, R. and ROBERTS, N. (1979) 'Autonomous study and

educational ideologies: A review of some theoretical and practical issues with special reference to the Schools Council General Studies Project', *Journal of Curriculum Studies*, 11, 1, pp. 53–67.

14. OETTINGER, A.G. (1969) *Run, Computer, Run: The Mythology of Educational Innovation*, Cambridge, MA, Harvard University Press.

Chapter 2

Students Active and Interactive:
A Question for Curriculum

The computer is an 'interactive' device. John Self defines this 'interaction' as that the computer 'can be programmed to react sensibly to what a user inputs'.[1] Once set up, we can communicate with it and make it respond to our behaviour. Properly programmed, it will play games with us, keep a score of our wins and losses, and tell us how long each decision took. It can run a programmed learning sequence, and shunt us along specific tracks according to our responses. Or it can be primed with all the information and rules for a simulation exercise, and help us design a fort, test a theory or diagnose a complaint. We can use it to explore possibilities — 'what if ...?' — without having to go through elaborate and time-consuming procedures, and the results will be useful so long as our initial assumptions and ground-rules were correct and properly input.

This is a remarkable facility, and it is little wonder that enthusiasts for computer learning make much of it. For Alfred Bork, for instance, failure to make use of the computer's interactive capabilities was the most serious weakness of poorly designed software, and he was not very impressed by 'extremely weak forms of interaction' such as multiple-choice questions. This interactive ability he contrasted with 'the passive learning modes that have been dominant for hundreds of years: books and lectures'.[2] A similar point was made by Rushby, that 'the book cannot detect whether the student is having difficulty ... and modify its approach to try a different strategy'.[3]

Well, certainly a book appears to stay the same whether or not it is read and no matter how it is read or by whom (though 'deconstructionist' followers of Derrida may disagree). A lecture seems much the same for all students, whatever each individual makes of it; it only 'interacts' if someone interrupts with a question. Whether the student is as active or passive as the teaching mode is another matter, to be explored in chapter 4. Meanwhile, Self reminded us:

> While computer programs are clearly more interactive than, say, television programmes, there are always limits on the kinds of thing a user can input and receive a sensible response to. Often the user does not know what these limits are. And the style of interaction is different from that between humans. . . .[4]

We can see the difference in that style of interaction if we suppose a student who gets either interested or confused by what the computer program is presenting and wants to ask a question. The lecturer can pause, hear the student's query, detect from the wording and the question itself the student's difficulty, uncertainty or interest, and give a helpful or reinforcing answer. Most books have indexes, and the student can either refresh uncertain memory, scan ahead to see how the point being made gets developed, or compare with another point made in a different chapter. When computer programs are in the Instruction mode, very little of this is possible. The interaction is one way. It is not entirely facetious to ask whether we prefer the computer or the student to be most interactive.

The 'Active-Passive' Continuum

No learning is entirely passive. As Gagné reminded us, running through all learning theories is the theme that:

> learning is, after all, an individual matter, *in which essential idiosyncratic elements must be supplied by the learner himself.*[5] (my emphasis)

Nonetheless, we frequently arrange the students into unidiosyncratic groups, and require only minimal responses, such as listening and copying. We find out by testing what specific pieces of information have been grasped as a result. What we know less about is what the student has learned about learning itself. The worry is that an unthinking passivity may be being encouraged or reinforced, and that learners may come to see learning as something done to them by other people.

Most teachers agree on the importance of 'motivation' and 'active involvement'. Both may exist even while the teacher is lecturing in the most didactic of modes, and the student who is apparently very 'busy' in activity projects may be totally uninterested and learning little. Nonetheless, one way of classifying teaching styles and learning modes is to look at the relative activity of teacher and student and particularly at who makes choices. Mosston[6] drew up a 'continuum of decisions in teaching methods', from 'Command' to 'Discovery', and much comment elsewhere appears to assume a similar model. Specific instruction, from teacher, worksheet, programmed learning unit or textbook, calls for a relatively low level of decision-making from the student, little initiative, little creativity. In a program as complex as that hinted at in the Rushby quotation above (for the feasibility of which see page 28) the student receives beneficial guidance but the key decisions are taken by the machine. Although in all such examples (and in viewing a film or reading a journal article) quite complex abilities are called upon from the student, it is all too easy for smaller or larger units of learning failure to develop. We don't know the cognitive model from which the student is working (and can the programmer always have anticipated the possibilities?); it may have only partial identity with what we had assumed and there are few chances for mismatches to be revealed: how indeed could they be? However in specific instruction the teacher is being very active indeed, aware of that activity, gaining personal satisfaction from it. In contrast to some of the learners, teacher is being purposive, making important choices and determining goals and objectives. 'The students must be learning: see how I'm teaching!'. And very often this is true, up to the point where the curriculum objectives call for or favour that kind of learning. Yet though the learner may have been intellectually busy, she or he has certainly not decided, not chosen, and perhaps not been personally committed or involved.

In theory at least, the degree of involvement goes up more sharply when participation is called for. This may be practical or experimental, setting up the means whereby a hypothesis may be tested or data collected: playgrounds are measured, weights dropped from a height, local residents questioned, particular terrains subjected to field-trip examinations. Hypotheses and concepts must be formulated, practical strategies planned, and manual and recording skills developed as well as analytic and judgmental abilities. Similarly with a library project (see chapter 3) — actively seeking information from a number of possible sources requires choice, decision, the possibility of initial failure, a revision of strategies and perhaps the comparison of conflicting evidence and the evaluation of credibility and bias. When practical information searches are brought together in a larger exercise, the student may have to set up ways of testing and finding out, incorporate items of found information from several different published or other sources, resynthesize into something new and different, and make judgments upon the result. Such activities were examined in Schools Council Curriculum Bulletin 9[7] and form the basis of much enquiry skills work.

Where does the computer come in all this? Abbott[8] urged that four main uses of computers in education represented a continuum, moving from Instructional through Revelatory and Conjectural to Emancipatory. This is very much what this chapter has argued. As Bork hinted, the degree of 'interaction' in computer learning varies enormously, but it is clear that he placed most value on that part of the 'interactive' continuum where the most thorough use of the interactive potential was made. But a careful distinction is necessary; just as teacher can be very satisfyingly busy (but the students only minimally involved) so with the computer. We need to ask: What is happening to the students? Are they simply responding to the prompting of the all-knowing machine, or does the learning sequence stimulate them to question back, in dual interaction, using the facilities of the computer to the full, not as master but as tool?[9]

Children learn from any teaching method, 'active' or 'passive', but may not learn the same things. There are many kinds of 'good' teaching but 'good for what?' and 'good for whom?' are the questions to ask.[10] As a very broad generalization we can probably say that specific units of knowledge are 'taught', by instruction, whereas their application and use is 'learnt', often by doing.

Thus, formal exposition is very effective for setting the scene, drill gives reinforcement and confidence (insecure students derive much comfort) and every teacher knows the value of a good formal session at mid-point, pulling together what has been learnt so far and ramming it home. Open-ended work gives the student a measure of choice in what is being done, and how, by what means and in what direction. It is a major factor (as we shall see) in the development of research skills, creative exploration and the ability to learn independently and 'make one's own meaning'. By contrast, when such work is chosen for the wrong purposes, or started without adequate organization and preparation, projects and open-ended work can waste time, lead to the experience of defeat and failure, and give precisely that disincentive to further effort which the teacher may have hoped to avoid. Somewhere between the two extremes is the kind of teaching that aims at stimulating the student to move from reception to active exploitation; most teachers see themselves as working in this middle way, with varying degrees of success.

By the time students reach the later years of schooling, they are purportedly being prepared for greater autonomy, particularly in 'A' level work and the supposed independence of university. But Martin[11] studied sixth-formers and found that in their first year of university it was the most independent who were often ranked by their tutors as problems, not thought likely to 'make the grade'. This is worth comparing with the more famous study, initiated by the late Lawrence Stenhouse from the University of East Anglia, which looked at how sixth-formers, their sixth-form teachers, and their own school (teacher-) librarians, actually saw the role of wide-ranging reading at 'A' level.[12] Not only was there no sign of the critical thinking and purposeful comparisons normally thought of as essential to 'A' level work, but also (and this now becomes pertinent to these pages) a major educational tool — the school library collection — was being used primarily as somewhere to sit while 'learning up' notes, its contents and its wider potential (for stimulating and enabling individual critical thinking) totally unexploited.

There are two reasons for criticizing software that under-exploits the interactive potentialities of the machine. One is purely economic: a costly resource is not receiving thorough-going use. This criticism is not unique to micros: ask any audio-visualist what he thinks of the typical use made by the average teacher of the opportunities provided by av media; ask school librarians how well their collections are integrated into curricular activity; ask experts in resource-based learning what they think of the typical use of worksheets. Alternatively, the charge could be more fundamental: that the missing interactiveness is itself of value, on the premise that good learning results when students are motivated to interact meaningfully with any kind of information source — including their own experience. But who is doing the interacting?

There is and may always be a shortage of really imaginative software programs[13] though one hopes that with further experience educational publishing may improve. Self[14] devastatingly criticized the current UK software scene and was suitably waspish about those who glibly assumed automatic progress. In a survey, the American Educational Research Association (AERA) graded six out of ten items 'not recommended' or 'do not consider' and only one in ten 'highly recommended'.[15] But there are many inferior textbooks around too, and studies showed[16] that 49.6 per cent of teacher-made *non-*

computer learning packages had 'serious problems' that limited their effectiveness. It is not unexpected if teachers value computer programs mainly for their ability to do what teachers themselves spend much time doing — controlling the students' learning and presenting specific units of information in challenging ways. But a teaching program that tries to replace the active teacher with the equally active computer does not come very far across the 'passive-active' spectrum and may be overlooking something important. There have been attempts to make books 'more interactive'[17], usually underestimating the active nature of reading in the first place (see chapter 4) and overlooking the fact that books are frequently consulted for purposes not anticipated by their authors. Such attempts show the traditional formal teacher's typical fear, that he may lose control over the learner. In contrast to the program where the computer knows all the answers, and the student must then find them, there is the more truly interactive use wherein the student uses the computer as a working tool for the creation of answers which they jointly discover.[18]

Whether or not this is desirable is not a technological matter: it is a professional decision based on professional questions. These questions are not 'Which format is most interactive?' but 'What is the nature of the interactiveness and what will it help me and my students to achieve?'. We ask (rather like Thurber's cartoon male, baffled by the inscrutable Marcia), 'What do you want to be interactive *for*?'.

A Question of Curriculum Purpose

How you teach alters *what* you teach, and what is *learnt*. Some discussions in education seem to assume that teaching methods are wholly interchangeable, taken off the shelf, dusted and used as a matter of pure convenience or personal style, or for the sake of variety, as if it was blindingly obvious that 'the modes of transmitting knowledge are transparent'.[19] This notion of 'transparency' is very pervasive. Experiments are designed in which painstakingly-matched classes are supposedly taught the 'same content' by two or more different 'methods'. Either the experimental design turns out to be faulty, with too many variables creeping in to give a clear verdict: or the design is so rigorous that the compared learning experiences are indistinguishable, with the unsurprising conclusion of 'no significant difference'. Tony Bates concluded that in evaluating the effectiveness of educational media 'most academic research has been totally unhelpful'.[20] It is hard to disagree, however devastating the implications.

We have to ask sensible questions about the very significant differences that do exist between ways of teaching.[21] This is what we have to ask about new information technologies: not to use them 'because they are there' but because of what they make possible, what unnecessary drudgery they cut out and how they alter what happens — and what we hope as a result the students will learn. Methods are not interchangeable and one cannot teach the 'same content' in two 'different ways' for the very obvious reason that the methodology changes the content. If we taught solely by chalk-and-talk, or solely through programs accessed by VDUs, this in each case would significantly condition the nature and content of the learning taking place.

In practice a variety of methodologies is desirable, because only through a variety of methodologies can all sensibly desirable objectives be met. It is not a matter of 'giving the students a change' or 'catching up with the marking backlog'. Teaching institutions priding themselves on being formal or informal are missing the point. The case against certain types of formal school is not that they teach what they do teach badly, but that there are other objectives to be tackled as well; the same was doubtless true of Summerhill and of many other 'progressives'. Thus one expects a close examination of the possibilities and a sensitive awareness of what is happening within and among the students, and this needs to be undertaken not only at specific points of teacher-student interaction (such as when Teacher X brings Concept Y to the attention of Class Z) but across the whole-school experience, in relation to both the specific and the overall aims of the curriculum.

Activity methods in education developed because of a mistrust of formal instruction, which included not simply the taught class followed by drill and questioning but also 'mere book learning'. Nowadays books are not the only problem; new media and computer enthusiasts could usefully join librarians in meditating for a moment on this quotation from Herbert Spencer:

> . . . only when his acquaintance with the objects and processes of the household, the streets and the fields, is becoming tolerably exhaustive — only then should a child be introduced to the new sources of information which books supply; and this, not only because immediate cognition is of far greater value than mediate cognition; but also, because the words contained in books can be rightly interpreted into ideas, only in proportion to the antecedent experience of things.[22]

To most of us, this rigid sequencing of long practice preparatory to reading (or any other 'second-hand' source) is unnecessarily extreme. We note the point — the importance of practical and meaningful experience — and try to arrange that the child's day contains a rich variety in which abstract and concrete elements blend.

The intimate personal experiences of taste, touch, smell, sight and sound, what happens when we do this and try that, are the basis of a great deal of our learning, and some of this can actually be experienced through the computer (that is the intention of LOGO, a language which combines growing understanding of the computer with experiences to deepen insight and spatial awareness). Social interaction, sharing the experience of others, can also be something in which the computer participates, because so much actual use of computers in the classroom is cooperative, children working in pairs or small groups around the keyboard and screen. We are social beings in a complex society, and much of what we 'know' (or believe that we know) has come from other people, in daily conversation and gossip, from what our parents told us, from radio and television and newspapers, from what we read in books and hear on record or cassette, and nowadays increasingly what we can access via the new information technology, including Prestel and its equivalents. We inhabit an entire world of information presentation which is as much a part of our daily lives as the weather, including the weather forecast.[23]

If we cannot truly separate the 'real world' from the 'mediated world', we simply have to teach understanding of both. In activity learning, the use of communication media is part of the activity; we are matching personal knowledge with 'shared knowledge', and as a result we gain greater control as well as greater understanding — we learn how to 'interact' with our world of experience and wrest our own meaning from it. Because knowledge is a social artefact, a study of how it 'presents' (to use medical jargon) is of the utmost significance. Herbert Spencer's practical experience is only a preliminary to the study of the wider universe which includes shared knowledge and record; if (as one head of geography told me, in tones that showed she expected praise) we 'keep the first-years away from books entirely' it will be so that books (and other media) may then be better understood and thoroughly used. It is clear from studies of unachieving readers that many of them have never really grasped the point of what reading is about, what a book could do for them or why they should try to learn to read it, and need that experience equally as much as that of 'objects of the household'.[24] For 'book' read 'television', 'computer', 'data networks' or whatever.

Most of us will be able to testify to the two-way flow: we become curious about something observed and want to read a book or see a film about it; but equally from seeing the film, or the TV programme, we look back at the living world with new understanding — and perhaps we buy the BBC book on the subject! Geographic fieldwork (to continue the argument) prepares us for the deeper study of geography that involves comparing a wide range of published accounts and data. No amount of fieldwork expeditions will enable children or university students to learn at first hand about continental drift. This latter is a marvellous example of how knowledge depends, not just on observation of the 'real world', but on the collection and collation of such observations. What began as a guess from the study of atlases, and spent long decades as a heresy, eventually emerged triumphantly as 'plate tectonics' when sea-bed studies demonstrated its persuasiveness. No-one unskilled in the sensitive use of 'shared information' could have reached such conclusions with such authority.

Nonetheless misgivings remain in many teachers' minds. We recall the charge made by the king in Plato's 'Phaedrus', on hearing of the invention of writing: 'This invention of yours will cause people to neglect their memory; they will gain a great deal of information without the wisdom to interpret it; and as a result they will be a menace to society.' Certainly the student who believes, 'It must be true because I read it in a book' will be led astray, but so may the seeker after truth who finds, not Socrates, but a bad philosopher. Suppose he or she turns to a program of computer assisted learning? In a ferocious issue of *Teachers College Record* in the summer of 1984, Douglas Sloan asked:

> What is the nature and quality of the sensory life encouraged by the computer? At what point and in what ways can the computer in education serve a vital, qualitatively rich feeling for life? At what points and in what ways will the computer in education only further impoverish and stunt the sensory experience so necessary to the health and full rationality of the human individual and society?[25]

Harriet Cuffard in the same issue worried that:

> ... the microcomputer introduces a particular learning style into the school setting of young children — the familiar posture of television viewing. The added dimension of interaction with the screen is small compensation when one

thinks of the usual, large-muscle, full-bodied movements characteristic of young children as they interact directly with the environment.

Her conclusion attacked not only CAL but more conventional methodology, including reading schemes:

> The question here is not 'Why use a microcomputer?' but rather 'Why use workbooks, animated or not, with young children?'.[26]

In later pages, Robert Sardello seemed to echo the 'menace to society' theme of the king in 'Phaedrus' by darkly forecasting that computer education would lead to 'a culture of psychopaths'.[27]

Such fears are grotesquely overstated, and fail to grasp the true possibilities of active learning through the computer-as-tool, as we shall see. Moreover, computer-based learning remains a very small fraction (1 per cent) of the total instructional system in the USA in any case. As with the old charge of 'mere book-learning', the answer must be that the danger is rarely with the format, but how that format is used. There is no reason in principle why the computer should be used uncreatively or why school experience should not be so organized that there is emotional richness rather than poverty. At present UK schools are organized so that nobody does any one activity to the exclusion of others; students move around, spend some time at the computer, some on the playing field, do lab work, listen to teacher, make things, write notes, consult books (rather briefly) and take part in art and music. Such variety can remain possible if teachers are in control, and so long as deschooling has not happened by edict or (more likely) by default. The development of the computer, which some hailed as leading to a brave new future of liberated learners, in fact requires us to place more emphasis than ever on schooling and the achievement of broad (as well as narrow) curriculum goals. Because each educational tool and methodology has the weaknesses of its strengths, so it is the job of education to see that students at risk are always appropriately helped — as long as the decision remains ours.

But we cannot abandon the tools that are properly available. There is a simple precept: The pupil must not simply be active in 'busy work' but interactive in the positive sense of quest for meaning.

Tools for Interaction

Many writers surveying current uses of the computer in education have sadly concluded that its forte is drill. They distinguish between reception learning and discovery learning and judge that CAL is at present best suited for the former. No instructional methodology exists that would allow us to acquire and use enough information about learners to provide ideally individualized instruction.[28] Indeed,

> ... even within a scenario of multiple machines and con-tinually improving software, the limitations of any program in anticipating the diversity of child responses and being able to assess appropriately partially correct answers or divergent creative responses will remain a significant conceptual bottleneck.[29]

Most predictions about CAL have been 'wildly optimistic'[30]; an in-built bias towards linear thinking has discouraged development of more complex and challenging materials, and the 'wholesome label' of 'interactive' all too often meant simply the computer saying, 'Try again, Johnny!'. Fothergill[31] with diplomatic caution doubted whether programmed learning was a viable way of teaching; there were elements of value but it might not be as widespread as all that. Self[32] made a simple calculation that with 100 frames to present and each frame branching to six other frames, this meant 10^{77} paths for the designer to ensure were available, assuming each frame was presented only once. Interpreting complex subject matter requires a detailed and interrelated knowledge of reality[33] and rule-following symbolic machines, however powerful they may be, do not have this knowledge.

Such disillusionment will not be surprising to those who have lived through previous educational revolutions. The initial euphoria of prophecy is followed by the increasingly cold shiver of realism: and if that was the end of the affair there would be no more to say. A broader, more optimistic reasoning would remain us that the past thirty years have seen quite astonishing technological developments, the pace of which has made it harder each year to think our way through. As Colin Baker reminded us, 'neither educational progress nor curriculum improvement is a direct and inevitable consequence of technological advance'[9]. We have been tackling uses of the micro-computer for much less than a decade, and it is hardly surprising if we have got little further than simple applications such as drill and straightforward transmission teaching.

If we keep our heads we shall notice that many teachers are quietly exploring other modes of computer use and reporting modest success. One example is LOGO, whose non-mathematical use is now being explored. Another such trend is the use of the computer in its word-processor mode as an aid to writing. Cheryl Liebling noted:

> ... the ability to use a computer does not minimize the importance of learning to read and write. To the contrary, the new technology complements print ... by providing exposure to yet another form of written language.... Unfortunately much of the software currently available consists of drill and practice exercises in which the computer serves as a consultant who knows all the right answers.[34]

She went on to investigate story-writing software packages such as Story Maker, and ways in which electronic mail systems allowed children to send messages to each other and to adults. Other teachers have reported favourably on such uses. Phenix and Hannan[35] found gains in confidence when children saw that writing could be manipulated, and print-outs produced end-products which others could actually read and enjoy. They concluded:

> When their writing was not limited by their ability to print and spell, the length, fluency and literary quality of their pieces increased. In turn, the quantity of writing led to a better familiarity with printing, and a development toward standard spelling. The computer proved to be a powerful tool in enhancing the children's composing and transcribing skills.

Despite the doubts which some will still express, this is clearly a very promising area to explore, using the computer as a tool for two-way interaction rather than for transmission teaching. Teachers value the microcomputer in primary schools as a tool and a teaching aid rather than as a replacement teacher, and emphasize the usefulness of games,[36] such as Microsoft's Adventure, for enhancing higher reading skills and presenting challenges.[37] This might be more convincing if the games were more imaginatively literate, and writing some would be a useful activity for an enthusiast. The information retrieval facilities of the computer present an interactive device for hypothesizing and testing, a tool for thinking with.[38] We shall see in chapter 3 that data gathered by students can be integrated through the computer and developed to produce displays, analyses and extrapolations, greatly enlarging the understanding of what has been found.

Simulations allow students to explore alternative possibilities, but their usefulness naturally depends on how well they are initially devised. A simulation is almost always a mathematical model with embedded assumptions about the nature of knowledge.[39] It has been questioned whether the pupil is really active in such contexts, and whether what was learnt could not have been 'discovered' from direct exploration of reality.[40] One is tempted to reply that a teacher who employs a computer simulation when reality is available as an alternative deserves every criticism. The earlier point is, however, well taken; we need a definition of 'active' that implies more than a tolerant tapping at keyboard and includes some degree of emotional and intellectual involvement, though again there is no reason in principle why a student should not feel 'involved' when working on a well-devized simulation exercise.

Teachers are commonly anxious to shift the focus of attention, away from 'learning as an achievement' or as 'a performance', and on to 'learning as a process'. Some helpful case studies by Nolan and Ryba concluded:

> ... the microcomputer's educational potential is more likely to be realized by conceiving of and using it as an instrument for learning rather than as an instructional system ... when students are permitted to interact with and manipulate a computer (i.e. exercise control rather than be controlled) then the computer learning environment will have profound effects on the quality of their learning and on their perceptions of their own ability.[41]

They called for a redefinition of the computer — 'an active medium through which various types of learning processes can be explored'. Such an approach is timely in view of other doubts: whether it will ever be feasible for publishers to produce educational software in the quantity and variety needed — bearing in mind that at present the total school market represents a tiny fraction of the overall software market and is insignificant beside the sum currently spent on textbooks and audio-visual materials.[42]

All these points will be nostalgically familiar to those who have followed earlier 'revolutions' in education. Resource-based learning was going to free the teacher from the transmission role, as the students learned from their own interaction with resource materials: but publishers and audio-visual producers were obviously unlikely to be able to produce the wide variety needed to match local curricula. So teachers would have to make their own (it would help them define need), and 'resource centres' became not only (or not so much) places for students but also print-shops and production agencies for teachers. Teachers who began idealistically with intentions of producing tape-slides or videos soon found the demands too heavy (especially as this coincided with 'the cuts' and the abolition of technician and librarian posts); and they sadly fell back on the quickly-produced worksheet and project booklet, sometimes partly made up of photocopied pages from the very books they (less competently) imitated. Similarly for many many decades the school library has been campaigned for as a potential medium for teaching and learning, yet a series of studies show that in the UK the school library has been generally neglected by teachers, relegated to a purely recreational function (which itself was regarded as expendable when times were hard) and that the creative possibilities of the information store and multiplicity of stimuli that such libraries present have hardly been examined.

It is difficult: a great deal of preparatory thought is necessary: things may easily go wrong. As a result, we lack a solid base of experienced theory on which to build our practice in the use of books and libraries, audio-visual materials, and now microcomputers: insufficient good programs — anyway it's hard to find out about them — and what happens if the machine won't function — and in any case, what is best practice and how do we know?

The practical side of this will be responded to in the final chapter, but the pedagogic questions lying beneath are arguably more important, in that we shall only use the technology effectively when we know how and why. The glimpses given above of the more imaginative approaches to IT will be followed up in later chapters, but as Sage and Smith wisely said:

> A great wealth of expertise has been amassed within the teaching profession, but the bulk of it is not supported by a systematic information base or by any depth of theoretical understanding.... There is no secure foundation of theory or even a hardcore of information on which future developments may be built. We have only the most inadequate basis for the design of the curriculum, or of educational experiences within its framework.[43]

Significantly they continued:

> Gutenberg's information technology revolution took place 500 years ago, yet even today many teachers apparently lack the skills needed to help children use printed works to best advantage.

and:

> Studies of investigative learning should have existing expertise in non-technology based information techniques on which to build.

The whole document is a call for further research, not into machines but their potential uses, for 'Modern technology supplies routes towards the achievement of the goal: it does not supply the goal'.

If one of the purposes of education is to pry the student free from passive dependence on the teacher (human or electronic) and develop the practice of active search and enquiry, then we need more from information technology than instructional programs. Because in these pages we are primarily concerned with 'the use of knowing', the next chapter will look at that most typical school example of the genre, projects, and try to rethink their nature in the light of the discussion so far.

Summary

To summarize chapter two:

1 The 'interactive' computer in the instruction mode can to some extent mimic the human teacher, responding differently according to how students behave. However, the enormous variety of such possible behaviours places human and economic limits on what programmers can sensibly forecast.

2 Thus although the computer can be helpful in both drill and programmed learning functions, these uses are relatively pedestrian, and prophecies of their widespread adoption seem unrealistic.

3 'Instruction' is in any case only one way in which learning is encouraged. Teachers usually develop a range of activities through which students explore and assimilate skills, insights and understanding.

4 The 'interactive' nature of the computer is increasingly being explored therefore as a 'tool for the learner' rather than as an 'alternative teacher' or even a 'teaching aid'. Students themselves interact with the computer (and with other learning resources) in a positive quest for the creation of meaning.

5 Such developments directly relate to 'the use of knowing' — the theme of this enquiry.

Notes

1. SELF, J. (1985) *Microcomputers in Education: A Critical Evaluation of Educational Software*, Brighton, Harvester Press.
2. BORK, A. (1984) 'Computers in education today — And some possible futures', *Phi Delta Kappan*, 66, 4, December, pp. 239–43.
3. RUSHBY, N. (1979) *An Introduction to Educational Computing*, London, Croom Helm, p. 38.
4. SELF, J. (1985) *op. cit.*, p. 29.
5. GAGNÉ, R.M. (1971) 'Learning theory, educational media and individualized instruction', in HOOPER, R. (Ed.). *The Curriculum: Context, Design and Development*, London, Oliver and Boyd for the Open University, pp. 299–319.
6. MOSSTON, M. (1972) *Teaching: From Command to Discovery*, Belmont, CA, Wadsworth P.C.
7. MARLAND, M. (Ed.). (1981) *Information Skills in the Secondary Curriculum: The Recommendations of a Working Group Sponsored by the British Library and the Schools Council*, London, Methuen Educational, (Schools Council Curriculum Bulletin 9)
8. ABBOTT, S. *Computer Assisted Learning in Geography*, unpublished BSc dissertation, Loughborough University of Technology.
9. BAKER, C. (1983) 'The microcomputer and the curriculum', *Journal of Curriculum Studies*, 15, 2, pp. 207–14.
10. JOYCE, B. and WEIL, M. (1972) *Models of Teaching*, London, Prentice Hall.
11. MARTIN, E. (1985) 'Conflicting ideals of dependence and independence between academic and library staff', *Education Libraries Bulletin*, 28, 2, summer, pp. 23–33.
12. RUDDUCK, J. (1984) *The Sixth Form and Libraries: Problems of Access to Knowledge*, London, British Library.
13. See, for instance BORK, A., (1984) *op. cit*; DAVID, P. (1983) 'Should there really be an Apple for the teacher?', *Times Educational Supplement*, 11 November, p. 13; DEDE, C. (1983) 'The likely evolution of computer use in schools', *Educational Leadership*, 41, 1, September, pp. 22–4; McCann, P.H. (1981) 'Learning strategies and computer-based instruction', *Computers and Education*, 5, pp. 133–40. A different view, that partly anticipates arguments in our later pages, will be found in: GOODYEAR, P. (1984) *LOGO: A Guide to Learning Through Programming*, Heinemann Computers in Education, pp. 30–1, 'The mythical software famine'.
14. SELF, J., (1985) *op. cit.*
15. KOMOSKI, P.K. (1984) 'Educational computing: The burden of insuring quality', *Phi Delta Kappan*, 66, 4, December, pp. 244–8.
16. FOX, A.C. and FRANKE, M. (1979) 'Learning centers: The newest thing in busy work?', *Reading Teacher*, 18, 3, March, pp. 221–6.
17. One example is DAVIES, W.J.K. (1975) *Learning Resources: An Argument for Schools*, London, Council for Educational Technology.
18. LIEBLING, C.R. (1984) 'Creating the classroom's communication context: How teachers and microcomputers can help', *Theory Into Practice*, XXIII, 3, summer, pp. 232–8.

19. ALVARADO, M. (1981) 'Television studies and pedagogy', *Screen Education*, 38, spring, pp. 56–67.
20. BATES, T. (1981) 'Towards a better research framework for evaluating the effectiveness of educational media', *British Journal of Educational Technology*, 12, 3, October, pp. 215–33.
21. ALVARADO, M. (1981) *op. cit.*
22. SPENCER, H. (1929) *Education: Intellectual, Moral and Physical*, Watts, p. 29.
23. One advocate of this point is KING, E. (1980) 'Education's steps towards computer-assisted learning', *European Journal of Education*, 15, 2, pp. 125–37.
24. FRANCIS, H. (1984) *Minds of Their Own: Recent Trends in Educational Psychology*, London, University of London Institute of Education, Professorial Lecture.
25. SLOAN, D. (1984) 'On raising critical questions about the computer in education', *Teachers College Record*, 85, 4, summer, pp. 539–47
26. CUFFARD, H. (1984) 'Microcomputers in education: Why is earlier better?', *Teachers College Record*, 85, 4, summer, pp. 559–68.
27. SARDELLO, R. 'The technological threat to education', *Teachers College Record*, 85, 4, summer, pp. 631–9.
28. McCANN, P.H. (1981) *op. cit.*
29. COLLIS, B. (1984) 'Implications of the educational use of computers in North American elementary schools', *British Journal of Educational Studies*, XXXII, 2, June, pp. 125–33.
30. SUHOR, C. (1983) 'Cars, computers and curriculum', *Educational Leadership*, 41, 1, September, pp. 30–2.
31. FOTHERGILL, R. (1981) 'How I plan to spend the money', *Educational Computing*, 2, 3, April, pp. 22–6.
32. SELF, J. (1985) *op. cit.*, p. 67.
33. DEDE, C. (1983) *op. cit.*
34. LIEBLING, C. (1984) *op. cit.*
35. PHENIX, J. and HANNAN, E. (1984) 'Word processing in the grade one classroom', *Language Arts*, 61, 8, December, pp. 804–12.
36. COATES, J.F. (1984) 'What principals should know about telematics, their impact on education', *NASSP Bulletin*, 68, 471, April, pp. 41–9.
37. MULLAN, A. (1981) 'Infant words and a sense of adventure', *Educational Computing*, 2, 11, December, pp. 49–51.
38. ROSS, A. (1984) 'Learning how to hypothesize: A case study of data processing in a primary school classroom', in KELLY, A.V. (Ed.). *Micromputers and the Curriculum*, London, Harper and Row, pp. 64–83.
39. O'NEILL, W.G. (1984) 'The educational potential of the microcomputer', *Computers in Schools*, 6, 4, pp. 120–4.
40. BAKER, C. (1983) *op. cit.*
41. NOLAN, P. and RYBA, K. (1984) 'The microcomputer as a learning system', *New Zealand Journal of Educational Studies*, 19, 1, May, pp. 24–33.
42. DAVID, P. (1983) *op. cit.*
43. SAGE, M.W. and SMITH, D.J. (1983) *Microcomputers in Education: A Framework for Research*, Social Science Research Council, pp. 18, 19 and 29.

Chapter 3

Projects: Knowledge Sought and Used

'Today, we have Naming of Parts.' A CAL program, a textbook chapter, or a talk-and-chalk class period, teach a specific subject area, as in Henry Reed's excellent poem. If the students master the specific content, or enough of it, then we judge the program, chapter or class session to have succeeded. Fit enough of these units together and perhaps you have an education system: what is missing?

Well, chapter 2 found that one missing element was student choice and decision: working actively rather than responding passively: practising skills: seeking and assessing information: and putting it all together in a finished product. If the finished product is large enough and the process long enough we call it a 'project'. In primary schools, it has been estimated[1] that children spend up to perhaps 15 per cent of their time on project or 'topic' work, frequently interdisciplinary in nature and intention. In secondary schools, projects of this kind may take place in the earlier years, or in general studies or humanities classes, but otherwise projects tend to be subject-centred, in (for instance) science, CDT, social studies or geography, producing models, experimental designs, lengthy reports or a 'folder'.

Here are four advantages of projects, from a list offered by Certificate of Secondary Education moderators:

Projects:
(a) allow pupils the chance to seek out information for themselves and use initiative in learning; . . .
(c) give the opportunity for information to be used rather than accumulated; . . .
(f) encourage the gathering and use of different kinds of evidence; . . .
(i) make pupils organize information into a coherent comment.[2]

Such activities are essential preparation for the 'new information society'. Suppose we remind ourselves of the kinds of question concerned adults seek answers to today. Here are some:

— Vaccinating my child: some press reports are different from what my doctor seems to say. What should I believe?
— I/we want to start a business but it seems dodgy. What are the pitfalls and what essential steps should we take?
— We think we should be exporting to X. What are the regulations, currency problems, political hazards, and will our product need to be modified or packaged differently?
— Our new neighbours, because of their religion, eat meat killed in a peculiar way. Why? Is it cruel? Is it safe for us to eat it?
— What difference will new information technology make to the way we live?

We get answers to most of these questions by consulting particular people, organizations and agencies, books and other printed materials, and in future it seems likely that computer services will carry more of the answers — and there will be different questions. Projects prepare us for finding answers to future questions and using the answers to some purpose. Considering the widespread nature of project work, there is remarkably little discussion of its implications in educational literature. More disquieting, much of what has been published could be described as the literature of inspiration and of intent, rather than precise description of achievement. Yet the essential elements of a project are in fact present in most assignments[3]; even to 'use a dictionary', the student must first, unless otherwise guided, make a choice of dictionaries (the simple one in his satchel, the more specialized or scholarly ones in the school or public library); struggle with alphabetical order, when perhaps the word's correct spelling is uncertain; and then plod through a numbered and confusing list of definitions (and sort them out from a clutter of data on pronunciation and etymology and past uses); and ask finally, 'Have I found the definition I really need?'. In the case of a scientific term, for instance, to have gone to a child's popular dictionary could have been disastrous and to a very advanced scientific dictionary wholly confusing. Good teachers anticipate these hazards and do not push students into choices they are not experienced enough to make. Electronic dictionaries won't be much different.

Objectives of Assignments and Projects

In '*Resource Based Learning*'[4] I listed some of the factors that were leading teachers to emphasize 'the need to encourage the student to develop as an independent learner and an autonomous enquirer' (p. 20). Ann Irving[5] put the key point succinctly and less pompously:

> The major problem faced by those for whom the information society will be the status quo is not that of acquiring information, but of rejecting the unnecessary and manipulating the essential.

Those are skills central to active project work. To many teachers however it is less than clear what they are or how they can be developed, within present constraints. Librarians are often on the receiving end of projects and persistently ask teachers (before, during or after) what was intended. What do teachers say, and what can go wrong on the way?

First: if as a teacher your main purpose is to 'get across' specific units of information, then a project or investigation is, to put it mildly, a very long-winded way to go about it. Many teachers assign high priority to 'covering the syllabus' in terms of its subject content, and feel they are working under considerable pressures to 'get them through the exam'. One group of teachers[6] gave a thumbs-down verdict on a resource-based programme for higher chemistry in Scotland for just this (predictable) reason. Yet experimental chemists themselves spend time on 'searching the literature', and LISC[7] reminded us that most examination syllabuses make rather more than token gestures towards skills and abilities beyond those of factual recall. Clearly, however, the message from the exam boards (if there is one) has not got through; we may argue about whether examination board syllabuses give adequate attention to investigatory skills, and whether written exams on the present model are suitable vehicles for testing their possession. We could change curriculum and examinations in order to change emphasis; we could reconsider skills learning, and (although the main purpose of teaching is learning) without listing what to assess we cannot ensure that students achieve what we hope from such changes.

The main purpose of project work is to develop skills and abilities in practice. Here are six useful abilities for a start:

1   To find and evaluate evidence (including discarding what is dated or irrelevant or suspect).

2   To come to a personal, independent judgment.
3   To participate constructively in group judgments.
4   To frame hypotheses, design tests for them, and justify conclusions from such tests.
5   To think shrewdly and creatively ('lateral', imaginative, speculative thinking).
6   To apply knowledge and experience to new situations.

Many of these skills will be taught as well as practised, at every level of schooling. Current interest in 'study skills' and 'information skills' has led teachers to analyze more closely the multiple sub-skills involved.[8] But like learning to swim, research skills need to be combined and regularly practised in realistic tasks: regular experience of enquiry and investigation is important in development. Even in specific subject areas, such as the interpretation of biological data, Simon found that regular practice sessions in the lab were essential: 'students cannot be taught how to interpret data by instruction alone'.[9]

A group of researchers[10] from Illinois explored strategies to improve students' performance and enhance learning abilities across subject areas. They advocated 'self control training' where the children were explicitly instructed in how to employ, monitor, check and evaluate their strategy; they warned teachers that 'strategies that promote recall . . . are not always the most appropriate for enhancing other learning outcomes'. One important finding was that children needed practice to develop their own psychological insights into what learning meant for them: 'they must know their own cognitive characteristics'. This is an academic way of describing the need to allow children to develop insight, including insight into something not often studied in school — themselves.

A Note on 'Discovery'

Such quotations emphasize the experiential and developmental importance of practical assignments and investigatory projects. To call the process 'discovery' or 'discovery learning' has I think been unhelpful, focussing on the wrong aspect, the student's progress through various unheralded 'Eureka experiences'. Arguments about 'discovery' are often woolly, the underlying logic fuzzy. Bruner[11] emphasized 'how one engineer's discovery makes it more workaday and less inspirational'; a very important part of *any* teaching. Enquiry learning and investigation are practice and process, where learning the route is at least as important as reaching one particular destination. Logically, a search procedure could lead to a *failure to discover*[12]: and one may criticize poorly structured 'discovery' projects for leaving students without counsel or prodding at just such moments. If discovery is 'a learner's goal-directed behaviour ... to complete a learning task without help from the teacher'[13] it is fairly obvious that:

> When the learner first makes the required response with little or no help from the teacher he may or may not have experienced 'insight', and he may or may not understand. Also he may have been acquiring some skills quite incidentally in the discovery process. Similarly, ... when the learner is memorizing it or practising it, he may still ascertain something new (to him) about that which he is practising.

If 'discovery' can happen in any context, then no one methodology is 'discovery learning'.

These objections only arise when more is claimed than evidence supports. By contrast, a well-known book urging primary teachers to explore 'topic work', made a different emphasis, stressing:

> that there is a range of intellectual skills, for example the skills of interpreting data, of giving arguments pro and con, of making judgments, *and that these skills can be cultivated* ... for example we would expect that children would acquire the confidence and the understanding of the nature of knowledge to be able to say on appropriate occasions, 'I don't know the answer to X. Maybe nobody knows it.'[14] [my italics]

If these are our aims, we can plan for them, and we must be able to ascertain whether we are succeeding. Active enquiry projects are not the philosopher's stone and it would be foolish to claim that their purpose is a magical and fortuitous moment of 'discovery' whose arrival we cannot predict. By analogy, a beginning student in the woodwork room perhaps 'discovers' what the experience of making a wooden object is 'like', and at an appropriate stage of development and learning may be able to plan a strategy for making ambitious objects, but not usually at the start. He or she explores and masters progressive skills, in preparation for greater autonomy, and en route makes items in which one hopes pride can be taken. Geography students may work steadily at CAL programs that begin with drill and increasingly move to exercises where choice and decision is necessary, but as this happens the work becomes increasingly project-like. Any assignment or project has the student going through a procedure or a set of procedures leading towards an eventual end-product, and the teacher's emphasis in planning will be on the procedures, with the end-product as a useful and necessary pretext for their practice. Chapter 2 looked at the 'active-passive' classification in terms of what a student actually did (including what choices were made) rather than at any spectacular illumination that might arrive en route or at the end. Such was the basis of Mosston's analysis of the range of teaching possibilities and his hope that we would move in a planned fashion from 'command' teaching toward, for example, 'problem solving'. Joycean 'moments of Epiphany' may indeed happen (in any teaching method) but though we can help to maximize the chances of their occurrence and the range of possibility they might cover, we cannot order or predict when or how such occurrences will transpire.

In that sense, projects are 'instructional', inasmuch as their planning has included a clear set of objectives, a reasonable analysis of what the teacher hopes may be learnt, both skills and concepts, and was conceived in order that these objectives might be achieved. I am, of course, using the word 'objectives' in a wider sense than the narrowly 'behavioural' model beloved of 'systems approach' devotees.

It is exactly in this wider sense however that Alistair Ross[15], writing from primary school experience, was able to assert:

> My experience using data-processing techniques with children is leading me to the conclusion that, with the necessary tools, young children are capable of working in a hypothetico-deductive manner, and that this could fundamentally change the pattern and direction of many primary school projects.

When children, of any age, work in such a manner, they are certainly 'learning to discover' — if we plan properly.

How Should the Teacher Prepare?

Enquiry projects are practical tasks developing learning skills. Some skills, as we have indicated, can usefully be 'taught' beforehand, and revised quite formally at appropriate points in the practical pro-gramme: if for instance it becomes clear to the teacher that students are floundering or unnecessarily wasting time. Some computer programs claim to teach specific enquiry and study skills, and these should be examined for their relevance by the teacher. If a suitable program is found it can be available as a resource. Learning strategies should be taught directly and practised regularly and indirectly throughout the school.[16] But only by a more than indirect practice will students learn to put all enquiry skills together and gain confidence in their use. Once clear on the skills (and the hazards) we can plan helpful structures for their practice, and unless we plan our students are unlikely to pick them up by instinct or happy accident.

Some teachers bridle at the thought of structured projects and feel the idea is a contradiction. Primary teachers in particular like a project to arise 'spontaneously' from the children's own interest, and seem to imply that in such cases it cannot be 'pre-planned'. This surely underestimates professional teaching judgment. If we have thought through in detail (and experienced ourselves) the purposes and likely processes, we can ensure that a framework develops usefully even in quite spontaneous enquiries. Then time will not be wasted on 'busy work'; that 'failure to discover' will be avoided or resolved (it can actually be helpful to fail on occasion; students need not always be shielded from reality).

How one structures depends on one's understanding of the implications of the assignment or the project. HMI once found in Dudley:

> The majority of the classes do work based on themes or topics, which is often geographical or historical. *Few schools plan the programme carefully so as to include a range of skills and concepts from different aspects of the curriculum.* In those which do the work is of good standard.[17] (my emphasis)

This comment is usefully interdisciplinary, countering 'tunnel vision'.

The skills and concepts can helpfully be listed and grouped in some meaningful way, and this is more than a one-teacher task. Marland[3] called for a whole-school curriculum on information skills and some schools have met in conference to look at what such a policy might imply. The difficulty is to be sufficiently detailed and specific without misleading or totally terrifying the teacher (some American school districts have produced thick tomes specifying stages in the acquisition of information skills and study skills from kindergarten to senior high). From Queensland, Bartlett[18] gave a detailed account of planning and developing what was apparently a state-wide programme of 'enquiry learning' in geography; his study emphasized (as it should) the importance of teacher understanding of enquiry learning methodology, which he described as 'inimical to traditional forms of learning by didacticism and recitation'. So Queensland teachers were given helpful documentation to guide their thinking; yet he noted that they 'invariably felt constrained to "cover" the subject matter content'. If this was not the intention, obviously the documentation did not make the context of their work sufficiently clear. So we must look at what enquiry activity might be expected to achieve — not in terms of 'subject content coverage' but of the abilities called upon and practised.

We listed on pages 37–8 six general abilities practised during projects. The 'nine steps'[19] give a helpful framework, not only for students engaged in enquiry but also teachers envisaging the likely progress of research and the hazards that might arise en route. As in all the best planned processes, we start with analyzing our objectives:

The Nine Question Steps

1   What do I need to do? (formulate and analyze need).
2   Where could I go? (identify and appraise likely sources).
3   How do I get the information? (trace and locate individual resources).
4   Which resources shall I use? (examine, select and reject individual resources).
5   How shall I use the resources? (interrogate resources).
6   What shall I make a record of? (record and store information).
7   Have I got the information I need? (interpret, analyze, synthesise, evaluate)
8   How should I present it? (present, communicate).
9   What have I achieved? (evaluate).

Some of the key questions which the teacher will ask in preparation for an assignment or an investigatory project follow logically from the above and can be asked before any specific project is contemplated; if you have a fair idea of the major implications it is easier and quicker to apply them to a particular instance. I suggest:

Key Questions for Teacher-preparation

1   What skills and abilities are called for at each stage of this work? (A careful list helps)
2   What links can be made to skills and abilities developed in other subject areas? (Maths, English and Creative Arts are three likely areas to examine but there may be others)
3   What problems may arise en route, which could:

    (a)   be avoided by good planning (for example, availability of books or equipment, access to people, bottlenecks caused by bad timing)

    (b)   require teacher intervention, counselling and help?

4   How will students' use of these abilities be monitored and assessed in practice? How can I know if the exercise is succeeding in its main objectives?

Computer technology and teletext add further dimensions of possibility to enquiry assignments and projects: as sources of information and stimulus; and as tools for information analysis and transformation. We look at some examples on pages 47–8. But the key role is with the teacher, not with the tools: the teacher who sets the tone, establishes the parameters, prepares the materials or access to them, deals with the unexpected and by judicious monitoring ensures that the major objectives of the exercise are achieved. The first element, typically, is the adoption of a questioning technique — 'Why would that be?', 'What makes you say that?', 'Show me how you got to this point', 'If that's the case, what would you expect to find?', and 'Run it, and see if that happens'.

    Bibens[20] emphasized this in an analysis of 'enquiry work' and the teacher's role, repeating the usual reminder about the teacher serving 'as a learning consultant' rather than as a 'resident expert'. He gave eight points of advice to teachers. Several of these points it is dificult to imagine ever being effectively built in to a computer assisted learning program: for example,

3   Be prepared to accept any decision reached by a student, and through the use of question, guide him back in the required direction. . . .

6   Do not allow students to quit in the learning cycle when they have identified 'an answer'.

7   Look for ways of encouraging students to move beyond the search for 'the' answer.

Despite such doubts, however, computers will be a valuable part of enquiry work, when they are tools and not teachers, as we shall now see from the experience of many teachers.

Computers and Other Tools for Enquiry

Projects can make use of any of the following resources:

* lab, workshop, domestic science rooms or other practical areas of the school, by arrangement, for appropriate practical work;
* microcomputers, for specific related instructional programs, and for project-related activities such as organizing data or deriving further data from it, or planning, using graphics facilities, etc.
* audio-visual and reprographic materials (slides, videos, audio-cassettes) and equipment, especially cameras and tape recorders;
* print materials held in classroom collections;
* print materials centralized in the school library, whether for use by incoming classes or for individual borrowing;
* print, av and other materials, perhaps including computer programs, coordinated in a school library resource centre;
* Ceefax, Oracle, Prestel and other information sources accessed via vdu screen, whether in the library resource centre or elsewhere;
* immediate school surroundings and the neighbourhood, as subjects of study in themselves;
* people and services in the outside world, including parents, art galleries, information agencies, specialist societies, the public library, etc. (by arrangement or with consultation whenever practicable).

The above list places computer and teletext facilities in their context, but in fact they are likely to have an increasingly important role in this work because of their versatility: not only as information providers but also as tools for the transformation of that information into something new. Where access problems are overcome, the computer may in future hold the control program, with students returning from other exploration to feed in their findings stage by stage, sharing it by networking and getting rid of much unproductively boring transcription and recalculation. Increasingly, programs of this kind are being devized, and it is worth noting how much of their use involves activity away from the terminal, finding the data from elsewhere. Few would mourn if this saw the end of the project worksheet or booklet — so long as the replacement was more creative.

Choice of tool is not the first of the Nine Question Steps; the start is always diagnostic. However, some tools actually help that diagnosis. A teacher in MEd research might after initial thought choose to seek help from a specialist data bank, such as ERIC, or Psychological

Abstracts. The material covered would probably be also covered by other indexing services in printed ('hard copy') form, but ploughing through the years of such volumes would be exceedingly time-consuming and many types of enquiry virtually impossible. That is why on-line searches are so frequent in academic libraries, by telephone line to California or wherever the data bank is housed.

In such searches, the enquirer first has to tell the computer those headings from the system's thesaurus that define the area of enquiry (for example, PROJECT + INQUIRY + GEOGRAPHY + TEACH-ING METHOD + SECONDARY SCHOOL). The headings must be chosen with care and combined with understanding, to get the most precise and also the most economical results (remember the phone bill). The computer indicates how many items in its memory have been tagged as dealing in some way or other with one or more of these headings; it will also show how many items were tagged as dealing with all of them; if the number is too great the enquirer narrows the focus by adding further limitations (+ CLIMATOLOGY + RAINFALL). Eventually, a list of manageable size is defined and printed out — after which the articles or papers have to be obtained and read (alas, there are no short cuts at that point!). Researchers beginning a PhD often find such a procedure helpful; not only do they trace material for study, but also in the process they clarify their own ideas on what the research is about — especially if the computer search is done by a skilled librarian acting as counsel and intermediary. A common response at the end is, 'I came to you confused, but now I think I know what I am trying to do!'.

This process is also present in a 'natural language' search; we still have to choose what 'natural language' terms we try first, and be ready to switch if what is 'natural' to us turns out not to be what other authors in perhaps other cultures or periods are using. 'Connect-time', on the telephone-cable link, is and will be expensive. (Many writers on this subject gravely overlook the complexity and sophistication of the skills likely to be required if future technology is to be used economically in money and time.) Equally, it is common experience for researchers to find, by pure serendipity, material which indexing systems and natural language searches alike 'miss', usually because only a specialist with a particular bias and sensitivity for language relevances would see the connections.

Schoolchildren are learning, at their own levels, what are essentially similar enquiry processes, and there are already computer programs supposedly helping them to do so. The SIR program (Schools Information Retrieval project, British Library/Aslib) was one interesting but insufficient first step in interrogating computer data banks.[21] Gilman[22] was enthusiastic here but somewhat uncritical. Not only do most school libraries seriously lack stock: few have professionally competent subject catalogues or subscriptions to major indexing tools from which some enquiry skills could also be rehearsed. Why then use computer search techniques? The student will hardly be searching through several hundred thousand sources as with ERIC. One answer is that such experience prepares for later searching in adult life (for example, through Prestel-like services) learning uses and (importantly) limitations.

Judith Askey[23] in an upper school in Bedfordshire used Prestel in the school library with project activity, and also built up, in a cooperative project linking teacher, librarian and children, a data base of community information which was later used in regular work by the whole third year. Prestel was used as a source of information, a medium for learning, a means of communication, an example of IT in the real world, and a source of software. Otherwise 'we deny ... the opportunity to acquire skills ... to those pupils whose families can't pay'.

It is surprising how much material assiduous students do manage to glean from the most meagre provision. Inadequate and 'cuts-affected' school libraries and classroom collections are woefully supported by public libraries and information agencies equally denuded and short-staffed; and the newer information technology providers have more lucrative markets than education to provide for. Yet many typical projects offer a daunting task which one wonders if teachers themselves always fully understand; the 'impossible project' is by no means a figment of a disgruntled student's imagination. Even projects well-chosen for a particular level of attainment can contain 'bugs' and hazards. Marland[24] briefly analyzed the following: 'Choose three migratory birds, draw maps showing their journeys and write on what their lives must be like.' The reader may like to draw a flowchart of decisions and activities flowing from it, concentrating particularly on what can cause X to do well and Y to flounder despite their best intentions. Luck can play an uncomfortably large part in the final 'mark' unless the teacher is very perceptive. Project design and resource provision are therefore crucial in planning. They go together, and should unite teachers and resourcers — as I tried to show in *Resource Based Learning*.[25]

Step two also reminds us that not all data valuable for a project come in easily dissected units. If we are to develop the student's ability to feel sympathy, to think into the experiences of others, to imagine life outside his or her local reality, there will have to be more extensive use of books, pictures, short films and videos, individually accessed. The affective and imaginative side of project work is as important as the cognitive. Chapters 4 and 5 look into these points in more detail, but we might note that a good historical novel can be both cognitive and affective, and that most adults get their main notions of the world outside their immediate experience from television: we ought to have practice in using that medium critically and effectively.

The Computer as Project Facilitator

Latent among the nine steps (above) is the possibility and indeed desirability of different types of material being collected together and then transformed into something else (step 7 particularly). The computer can be very exciting here. The student who learns how to draw the migratory routes of his three birds on a map on the classroom or library micro is learning and practising many abilities at once and will probably have a considerable feeling of achievement as a result. In a historical or local project, different students can gather material from reference books, census records, gravestones and parish registers, pool what they find and feed it into an appropriately pro-grammed computer for display and analysis. Nature study observa-tions, multicultural surveys and geographic fieldwork also benefit from computer transformation. Ross[26] gives interesting accounts of how such material can be displayed in rank order charts, pie charts, histograms, and scattergrams for further analysis with the use of program packages now available, such as FACTFILE, LEEP, QUERY and PGQUERY.

The wide public interest in the raising of the Tudor ship *Mary Rose* led to the production of an interdisciplinary computer package, which many have found helpful as a project focus. Children were able to enter imaginatively into the experience of the team in finding, mapping and eventually lifting the different sections of the vessel, particularly combining mathematical and geographic understanding. (As much of my emphasis so far has been non-mathematical, this is perhaps a useful chance to stress the importance of a proper integration of number work into investigatory projects; a sound mathematical content need not preclude literary and artistic activity and may be a helpful stimulus to language development as children work out their problems collectively.)

The potential, if someone will help us release it, is great: to build data into results hitherto impossible in the classroom — genuine transformations without unnecessary chores or what Stephen Kemmis[27] calls 'inauthentic labour'. Such programs would be much more rewarding than a further proliferation of games or instructional units. There will be more possibilities still for this when the interactive videodisc becomes available to us at reasonable prices and in a permanent format, and many teachers are already looking forward to being able to make creative use of the 'Domesday' project material, developed in conjunction with the BBC, whereby among other things complete photographic records of the UK will be available and easily retrievable on disc.

Earlier I mentioned some general word processing uses of the micro, but it is worth adding the value of these in the building up of project reports, from scattered and unconnected sentences or paragraphs to completed texts which can be printed out neatly (with graphics) in a way the student or the class can take pride in. Building up text on a good word-processing system is quite a different activity from most people's conventional note-taking and drafting. Afterwards the printout in a neat folder can remain in the collection as a resource, or (more expensively) saved on a disc. This links to steps 5, 6 and 8.

Equally there is no reason why a project should not have an artistic dimension with a computer element. Graphics work, including uses of colour, is becoming better understood and is widely popular with young people as well as adult hobbyists. It teaches logic and creative design together. Similarly, the microcomputer's ability to produce music is improving rapidly (even if it still has some way to go) and the programming exercise can give analytical insights into time and pitch which usefully link with physics work. This may not be how music has been traditionally taught: indeed music could not have been taught in such a way because the technology did not allow. But some teachers will feel that the expressive and affective elements are not automatically destroyed by additional activity, and specifying a BASIC command such as ENVELOPE 1,1,0,0,0,0,0,0,2,0,−10,−5, 120,0 is not necessarily antimusical if the student knows what each element in the command actually means. Understanding of what music physically is may actually increase as a result (though it will not help us to enjoy the music better nor appreciate what it means or contributes to human life). I pass no comment on BASIC as a music-producing computer language — but there are others. Bamberger[28] has reported extensively on her work with LOGO and music students.

There is always the danger that students will turn, not to the resource most suitable for their purposes, but to the one they think it is most prestigious to use (or alternatively, the simplest they can get away with). The illustrations above are neither prescriptive nor exhaustive, and if the project is well chosen and planned its own logic should prescribe the tools and resources needed, as well as the skills practised. This again emphasizes how important it is that such activities be planned by or with an alert and informed teacher. This, however, means a teacher to whom project enquiry is a familiar exercise personally practised; the teacher who perceives himself as having only enough time to rummage briefly in the departmental textbook cupboard should hand over project planning to a colleague.

The Question of Participation

Only three of the nine-question steps actually have to do with handling and consulting resources; almost all the others are concerned with thinking, choosing, comparing and finally presenting: with, as I have called it, 'the use of knowing'. One teacher summarized two interrelated processes:

(a) *a search process* , in which a person attempts to determine where the desired information is likely to be located, and
(b) *an evaluation process* in which the suitability and sufficiency of gathered information for retrieval questions are determined.[29] (my emphasis)

This normally means that what is found is transformed into 'the answer': how well depends on the student, the project and the teacher. If all that is happening is the notorious 'just copying from books' then the exercise has been badly prepared and monitored by the teacher and should be redesigned for next time. If the micro can help here, all the better.

Sylvia Leith found a surprising failure in schools to come to terms with the problems of assessing project work (of which more on page 55), and commented:

A sceptic might be tempted to suggest that teachers use project work to help solve a management problem; it enables them to gain a breathing space within the very hectic setting of an overcrowded, demanding classroom.[30]

One can sympathize with the need for such breathing spaces without accepting that they should be gained at the expense of meaningful learning. But this is precisely where another challenge arises: How far is a project really allowing children to exercise genuine choice, if it has been arbitrarily pre-designed by the teacher?

Some critics have no doubt here: questions children are set are too often formulated entirely by their teachers so that the main motivating force — children's own driving curiosity — 'has been got rid of before the work is even under way'.[31] No doubt this sometimes happens but is it unreasonable to hope that most teachers know their classes sufficiently well to be able to choose or slant topics in ways that capture interest? Can it really be true that teachers lack the leadership qualities that help them to find ways of awakening such interest when it is not immediately present? Are such critics really only criticising bad teachers?

The problem with many youngsters is, sadly, not that they are given assignments which are uninteresting to them, but that they are locked in an apathetic mode wherein they are unable to conceive of anything being interesting at all. In the *Need to Know* project, Terence Brake[32] set out to counter this and at the same time introduce information skills; he devized enquiry sessions, resource based, geared to the social and recreational needs of his 16-year-old classes. The nine question steps remain much the same even when the problem is how to find out what movies or rock concerts are going on and how to get there. Other teachers have experimented with projects on social security entitlement and dealing with the job centre, or coping with football hooliganism, and other supposedly 'realistic' topics.

Computers are said to be 'motivating' and there may be occasions when the fascination of the machine may be worth capitalizing upon. But Self's comment is worth pondering:

> Most children enjoy computer games (and paddling in the sea) but this does not mean that the games 'engage motivation', as most commentators seem to assume ... *a pupil is motivated when he identifies with the objectives to which learning leads.* Computer games are alluring, involving, even addictive, but they are not necessarily motivating.[33] (my emphasis)

He goes on to ask if it matters, so long as the pupil learns?

> Maybe not, if we are happy to teach by deception, that is, by introducing activities whose motive is something other than that appreciated by the pupil.

But this overlooks the motivating factor of having a tool that truly enables one to do meaningful things. We are not 'teaching by deception' if we use the computer in a way that stimulates the pupil to think independently and often in a way the teacher has not known enough to expect.

Some teachers try to capitalize on the latent idealism of youth and their readiness to be involved in meaningful environmental investigation. The Ottawa experiment was one example: a continuation of the Naples/Oxford 'Community Participation by Children in Futures' project, or Gruppo Futuro[34]. Between sixty and seventy Ottawa children, spurred by Simon Nicholson of the Open University and two colleagues, were set to examine Ottawa in the present and plan meaningful future changes. Over five days using cameras, audio-cassettes, murals, 3D sculpture and planning 'futures books' they produced a wealth of ideas, materials and media which later formed part of 'an international, adult-dominated' conference for the International Year of the Child. McDevitt commented:

> The children came to realize that the future is in their hands. They mould the future as they see fit. Hopefully they will learn from the triumphs and failures of the past and with a look at their needs will design the future to best accommodate their lives. The children truly felt like people with a real purpose. They were the decision-makers.[35]

This sort of enthusiastic reporting matches an exercise in a similar subject area, in the UK: an environmental project using the 'Living Space' pack. This was developed with the help of a workshop group of teachers in primary, secondary and further education, and distributed by Education for Neighbourhood Change, from the University of Nottingham School of Education.

> We wanted to change from the way in which some teachers were accustomed to use 'audio visual materials'. Instead of using them mainly to reinforce the teacher's exposition, we wanted our materials to support children's own problem-solving and decision-making, working together as mixed-ability groups.

The materials were used in some 200 classrooms in eight different local authorities in England and Scotland over a four-year period. There were two versions of the pack: in the 'instil' and 'elicit' modes respectively. Teachers using the 'instil' mode reported that 'as usual' after a few weeks class interest began to wane; whereas with the 'elicit' mode teachers were amazed at 'the staying power, the self-reliance, the self-discipline, of their children'.

In many instances the school project linked up with community action in the neighbourhood and participated in the decision-making of adults.

> ... children's interest in number work, map work and language was dramatically increased because they needed these skills in order to get on with the purposeful activity their project generated.[36]

Such enthusiastic accounts arise from time to time in the literature, and it would be foolish as well as churlish to ignore them or sneer. What one misses (and this is true of much of the literature on projects) is evidence of something more than a simple description of enthusiasm. In today's hard world one has to convince people for whom enthusiasm is insufficient, including teachers who like to feel that an enthusiastic class has also achieved something modestly measurable. If number and map work improved, it ought not to be impossible to give at least a general idea of by how much, or at the very least how this became apparent. Meanwhile, what of other skills and abilities? How can a cautious teacher wishing to experiment get a general idea of whether the various skills of enquiry are really being learnt, and by everyone? Well, Nicholson says,

> People often ask ... 'how do you evaluate what you do?' Most people remain unaware that they can query the question.... It does not occur to many adults that children are capable of evaluation and that when they invent and make things organic evaluation takes place as part of living.[37]

It is possible to take his point and yet to feel that this does not preclude the adults also having a view, and an informed one, which might be of value to other adults contemplating similar work.

To Assess the Unassessable

'Well, that was fun, wasn't it!' Many will feel uneasy if this flip sentence is the main summary of (say) three weeks of project work.[38] Of course there is no reason why learning should not be fun — so long as it is learning. But we ought to have some measure of whether the project (as well as the student) has been successful.

This emphasis is important, because assessment has different purposes. Some teachers and schools use assessment to be able to produce regular 'league tables' of students' achievement in competition with each other, to encourage continuing effort or reassure parents. Others give the student a mark as a signal of personal achievement ('That piece was at B+ level'), irrespective of what other students are 'getting'. In many ways a more important purpose of assessment is to give the teacher as clear a guide as possible to the success or failure so far of the chosen teaching method. This is surely the answer to those who, like Deale, suggest that the value of project work would remain even if it were not assessed at all.[39] Quite apart from any motivating value for the student, the teacher always needs an analytical tool to monitor whether (and which) teaching styles are resulting in learning. The question is how this can be found out (what would we be looking for?), and the problem is how to do it without fatally injuring the project in the process.

This point is made in a thoughtful analysis by Deere[40] who reminds us that 'because in project work the teacher is linked firmly into the process ... the final assessment is as much a measure of him as it is of his students'. Whereas a short assignment can be relatively clear in its challenge and requirements (and yet often have unforeseen complexities in practice), the many-sided nature of project work makes assessment very difficult. Deere emphasizes four points:

— an ill-chosen assessment scheme 'undermines the whole notion of project activity';
— the teacher is inevitably part of the resulting work because few if any projects entirely exist without teacher guidance;
— it is not possible to distinguish between the teacher's various activities as planner, consultant and assessor;
— the very nature of project activity produces a wide range of variables which lead in turn to a range of 'acceptable and often unforeseen solutions'.

Even supposing the teacher can disentangle his or her own different roles within the exercise, the individual nature of many projects means that what one student has had to tackle may in no useful way resemble the challenge overcome by another. Take some likely instances: student A draws up a careful questionnaire and (despite shyness and a stammer) gathers a great deal of information from a selected sample of the general public; student B works out a remarkably complex BASIC program (so far as anyone can tell, without help or crib) which radically affects the class's ability to present its final conclusions effectively. Student C produces a wealth of information, neatly indexed on 5 × 3 cards, but has a mother who works as Reference Librarian in the local public library. Students D and E elect to work together, despite their very different levels of achievement throughout schooling; they turn in identical pieces, and E's is spelt correctly for the first time in living memory, but both include data on homing pigeons which are E's only known passion and in which up to now D has shown no interest whatever.

Clearly a traditional marking system is inadequate either as a guide to the student or as a measure of the teacher's effectiveness or that of the chosen methodology.

Deale[41] suggested assessment under presentation, research, content, and conclusion, and proposes differential weightings under each, depending on the special circumstances of each exercise. We may however need to start differently: to separate process from product and assess each quite separately. If we want specific enquiry skills to be learnt and practised during the exercise, then their use must be in some way clearly articulated for assessment and well weighted by the assessor. An end product which does not reveal such matters is not helpful. Either the rules for the final presentation must be so prescriptive that the points to be assessed are forced to appear — (which may be impossible or demotivating); or else evidence of process must come in other ways, perhaps from a roughwork diary of activity, regularly seen and checked by the teacher, or by oral interview, at the end or at various stages en route. The advantage of separating process assessment from that of the end product is that the student may be encouraged to produce a 'project report' (or whatever) which can be prized for itself, without containing laboriously tedious 'first I did this, then I looked up that' entries whose proper place is elsewhere. This product can receive an appropriate mark. Meanwhile the teacher can keep a record book of some kind for skills achievement and any other comment, quite separate from a public mark schedule and largely there for the teacher's own guidance.

The labour involved in this sort of record keeping is not of course inconsiderable, and likely to be a disincentive to the weary teacher, already under severe pressure from elsewhere. As Davies[42] put it, in coursework and project the teacher has to work out:

> the best way to test a particular skill, situation or pupil; how frequently to test; how to evaluate the results and how to use them. . . .

Defining a project as a 'decision-chain model consisting of three phases . . . the initiation of the project, its course as it is pursued, and . . . its terminal result' he analyzes the problems involved, noting the crucial nature of the initial choice of topic, which if ill-chosen can 'destroy the whole value of the technique'.

Haggitt[43] also suggested a virtual process/product differentiation in that 'the teacher's records should show how children are moving through a sequence of activities and also what concepts they are acquiring'.

Some guidance offered to the teacher however seems to create resistance, and one can be forgiven for a sneaking sympathy. In 1978 the ORACLE project produced a checklist of objectives for project work, including forty-seven criteria for assessment, under eight main headings; Leith undertook to test the use of this list in nine urban and rural schools with thirty-seven teachers, each of whom had expressed an interest in participating. Two terms later, none had used the checklist. The reasons were wide but predictable. Leith commented:

> Perhaps the answer is that all teachers using the project method need to develop their own sets of goals including skill and content objectives for each project the children attempt, and then, based on these, develop a simple assessment scheme.[44]

Professionalism surely requires more than either guesswork or shoulder-shrugging resignation, but should steer clear of over-kill.

Education has traditionally emphasized the assessment of content mastery and recall, so perhaps it is not wholly surprising that few schools seem yet to have worked out a whole-school policy on skills acquisition. Yet this is particularly regrettable, given the interdisciplinary nature of skills work and the growing importance of their successful mastery in any likely future society. I suspect that individual teachers would have fewer problems in assessing the success or otherwise of their work in this area if there were more helpful and understandable guidance policies. If, as has already been suggested, the school as a whole worked out its 'information skills curriculum', making the integration of such skills into lesson planning part of the everyday life of the school and their monitoring part of ordinary assessment, classroom teachers would be less isolated, members of a community that agreed on at least the minima that needed recording. We will look at the contribution that could be made by examining boards in the final chapters. Nevertheless we need to remind ourselves that what we teach as 'knowledge' is 'knowledge-now'; it is necessary in order to deal with the immediate problems of 'learning-now', and as a useful structure within which to learn and practice methods of learning, skills of learning and enquiry, and move towards self-confident autonomy as learners. Students need that confidence and that autonomy for another context, the changing future in which they will spend the rest of their lives; during this time they will find that the 'knowledge-now' we gave them is shifting and transmuting; it becomes a succession of 'knowledges-then'. Active enquiry and project work is important precisely for that time. The next chapter continues the study.

Summary

Thus we can summarize chapter 3:

1   The main purpose of projects is to practise and develop skills of finding and using relevant information to create a larger and meaningful product. Personal involvement, problem solving, hypothesis forming and testing, and information retrieval skills, all play their part. There may be useful attitudinal and imaginative spin-offs.

2   Projects should not be used when the prime objective is the quick acquisition of subject content: neither should 'resource based learning'.

3   The microcomputer, among a wide range of other infor-mation sources, will be increasingly helpful for presentation, informational retrieval, and the manipulation and transformation of data collected.

4   The microcomputer may well carry the main instructions for the project, and give the teacher a major tool for control and structure. The final product may also appear on the computer, but this depends on what the project is about.

5   In the design and oversight of projects, teachers will find the 'nine steps' helpful as a framework for most enquiry work. These will need interpretation in context.

6   The skill of the good teacher ensures that a project captures the interest of students and relates to matters of concern to them. The supposed 'motivating force' of the computer is only educationally relevant if it relates to educational purpose, including the students' acceptance of the goal of the enquiry.

7   Projects are a means to an end; teachers need clear ideas on skills and concepts to be developed and ways in which they can judge how far these have been attained. Assessment must

never get in the way of learning, but the teacher must be able to judge how successfully the students are reaching the eventual goal of confident autonomy as learners and enquirers.

Notes

1. LEITH, S.(1981) 'Project work: An enigma', in SIMON, B. and WILLCOCKS, J. (Eds) *Research and Practice in the Primary Classroom*, London, Routledge and Kegan Paul, pp. 55–64.
2. HOSTE, R. and BLOOMFIELD, B.(1975) *Continuous Assessment in the CSE: Opinion and Practice*, London, Evans Methuen (Schools Council Examination Bulletin 31), p. 72.
3. MARLAND, M. (Ed.) (1981) *Information Skills in the Secondary Curriculum: The Recommendations of a Working Group Sponsored by the British Library and the Schools Council*, London, Methuen Educational (Schools Council Curriculum Bulletin 9).
4. BESWICK, N.W. (1977) *Resource Based Learning*, London, Heinemann Educational Books.
5. IRVING, A. (1982) 'Information retrieval in education — A worthy tradition?', *Computer Education*, 41, June, pp. 15–16.
6. WHITEHEAD, R.S. (1984) 'Resource based learning: Innovation or bandwaggon', *Scottish Curriculum Development Service, Dundee Centre Journal*, 26, November, pp. 44–8.
7. Office of Arts and Libraries, Library and Information Services Council. (1984) *School Libraries: The Foundations of the Curriculum*, Report of the . . . working party on school library services, London, HMSO.
8. See, for instance IRVING, I. and SNAPE, W.H. (1979) *Educating Library Users in Secondary Schools*, London, British Library Research and Development Dept.; MARLAND, M. (Ed.) (1981) *op. cit*; TABBERER, R. (1984) 'Introducing study skills at 16 to 19', *Educational Research*, 26, 1, February, pp. 1–6.
9. SIMON, E.W. (1980) 'Learning to interpret data', *Journal of Biological Education* 14, 2, pp. 132–6.
10. BROWN, A.L. (1981) 'Learning to learn: On training students to learn from texts', *Educational Researcher*, 10, 2, February, pp. 14–21.
11. BRUNER, J. (1972) *The Relevance of Education*, London, Allen and Unwin, p. 80.
12. CLARK, C. (1979) 'Ausubel on discovery and verbal learning', *Educational Philosophy and Theory*, 11, March, pp. 1–15.
13. KERSH, Y. and WITTROCK, M.C. (1970) 'Learning by discovery: An interpretation of recent research', in STONES, E. (Ed.) *Readings in Educational Psychology: Learning and Teaching*, London, Methuen.
14. GUNNING, S. (1981) *Topic Teaching in the Primary School,* London, Croom Helm.
15. ROSS, A. (1984) 'Learning how to hypothesize: A case study of data

processing in a primary school classroom', in KELLY, A.V. (Ed.) *Microcomputers and the Curriculum*, London, Harper and Row, pp. 64–83.

16. BRIEN, R. (1982) 'Strategies for change: Learning to learn. Suggestions for the development of a curriculum at the high school level', *Programmed Learning and Educational Technology*, 19, 3, August, pp. 219ff.

17. Department of Education and Science. (1978) *Educational Provision by Dudley Education Authority: A Survey by HM Inspectors of Schools*, London, HMSO, p. 23.

18. BARTLETT, V.L. (1982) 'To evaluate an inquiry learning program in geography', *Geographical Education*, 4, pp. 35–50.

19. MARLAND, M. (Ed.) (1981) *op. cit.* For a fuller examination of the implications, see IRVING, A. (1985) *Study and Information Skills Across the Curriculum*, London, Heinemann Educational Books.

20. BIBENS, R.F. (1980) 'Using inquiry effectively', *Theory Into Practice*, XIX, 2, pp. 87–92.

21. ROWBOTTOM, M.E. (1983) *The Schools Information Retrieval (SIR) Project*, London, British Library, (Library and Information Research Report 15).

22. GILMAN, J.A. (1983) *Information Technology and the School Library Resource Centre: the Microcomputer as Resourcerer's Apprentice*, Council for Educational Technology, (Occasional Paper 11) (see p. 146)

23. ASKEY, J. (1985) 'An information frame-up', *Times Educational Supplement*, 26 April, p. 9.

24. MARLAND, M. (Ed.) (1981) *op. cit.*

25. BESWICK, N.W. (1977) *op. cit.*

26. ROSS, A. (1984) *Making Connections: Developing the Primary School Curriculum Using a Computer for Information Retrieval*, London, Council for Educational Technology and Microelectronics Education Project (MEP Case Study 5).

27. KEMMIS, S. (1977) *How Do Students Learn?*, working paper, Norwich, University of East Anglia (Centre for Applied Research in Education)

28. BAMBERGER, J. (1982) 'Logo music', *BYTE*, 7/8, pp. 325 and 328.

29. KOBASIGAWA, A. (1983) 'Children's retrieval skills for school learning', *Alberta Journal of Educational Research*, XXIX, 4, December, pp. 259–71.

30. LEITH, S. (1981) *op. cit.*

31. MERRICK, J. (1970) 'Children, books and things', in University of Exeter Institute of Education, *The Library and the Changing Curriculum: Proceedings of a Conference*, 7–20 September, pp. 26–40.

32. BRAKE, T. (1980) *The Need to Know: Teaching the Importance of Information: Final Report*, January 1978–March 1979, London, British Library Research and Development Department.

33. SELF, J. (1985) *Microcomputers in Education: A Critical Review of Educational Software*; Brighton, Harvester Press.

34. NICHOLSON, S. (1980) 'Child participation in futures: The Ottawa experience', *BEE*, 108, April, pp. 13–17.

35. McDEVITT, K. (1980) 'It's up to us....' *BEE*, 108, April, p. 13.

36. The two quotations from an unattributed full issue of *BEE*, 109, May 1980.

37. NICHOLSON, S. (1980) *op. cit.*

38. KENT, G. (1968) *Projects in the Primary School*, London, Batsford, pp. 31–2.
39. DEALE, R.N. (1975) *Assessment and Testing in the Secondary School*, London, Evans Methuen (Schools Council Examination Bulletin 32).
40. DEERE, M.T. (1974) 'The assessment of project work', in MACINTOSH, H.G. (Ed.) *Techniques and Problems of Assessment*, London, Arnold, pp. 102ff.
41. DEALE, R.N. (1975) *op. cit.*
42. DAVIES, P. (1979) 'Coursework and projects', *Secondary Education Journal* 9, 3, November, pp. 12–14 and 20.
43. HAGGITT, E.M. (1975) *Projects in the Primary School*, London, Longmans.
44. LEITH, S. (1981) *op. cit.*

Chapter 4

Three Literacies for a World of Change

Reading: What the Computer Can and Cannot Do

Not every teacher, surveying computer research in education, has asked Bracey's question, but it seems a good one:

> ... what good would it do us to have the most efficient method of teaching reading ever devised if no-one taught by it ever picked up a book?[1]

Of course, reading is not limited to a single mode or to one format: we read posters, labels, blackboards, magazines, signposts, invoices, memoranda, overhead transparencies, books in hardback and paperback, loveletters and computer screens — among many others — and certainly the paperless society forecast by futurologists will merely transfer our reading activity from one medium to another — if it ever arrives. Even if we have computers which recognize spoken commands and reply in kind, there will still be much else that only the ability to read will make meaningful. Recorded information and communication in an extended format seems unlikely to become unnecessary; it may change its manner of presentation (and has done so before) but we shall still need to access something essentially 'a book'. And if we have a choice of format — for instance, to read the 608 pages of Bullock's *A Language for Life* on screen, or to have it spoken to us by a talking computer, or to have it in print form — there is little doubt which most people would prefer.

The book is itself a piece of technology (rendering obsolescent the memories of professional bards), and in recent decades that technology has been supplemented by the movie film, sound recording, broadcasting, video and the computer, including teletext and (just arriving) the interactive videodisc. As a result we have diversified our activities; much of the time we once spent reading novels, we now devote to TV and video (and read novels in bed or on journeys). Salespersons prefer to use videos rather than glossy brochures; accountants feed figures into computers rather than ledgers; motor mechanics check spare parts on fiche rather than handbook. But the importance of literacy as a major accomplishment of the educated person has not in the least diminished; it has merely been added to by further requirements — sometimes called 'visual literacy', 'media literacy' and 'computer literacy'.

Writing remains the major medium of understanding. As Lacy put it:

> Meaning is a phenomenon created by the reduction of experience into words organized in sentences. The process of understanding is the very process involved in reducing an event to writing.[2]

And 'reading' has become a synonym for active (or perhaps interactive) study. Paulo Freire explained:

> I am referring to the fact that 'reading' the universe must always precede reading the word, and reading the latter implies continuity in 'reading' the former. This movement from universe to word and back again is always present in literacy teaching.[3]

Whatever else reading is, it is not reducible to a mere 'barking at print' or decoding a set of squiggles into a set of sounds. It is a cognitive process in which the contributory activity of the reader is crucial: sampling, predicting, testing and confirming. While readers are reading they are simultaneously processing and using many different types and levels of information: for instance, letter shapes, the syntactic arrangement of words within sentence or paragraph, the sensed pattern of meaning apparently emerging, and the accuracy or otherwise of guesses made about what will come next. It is a very active process.

Not only are we occupied, in reading, with continual retrospective understanding (so that READING changes its perceived nature when we turn the page and find that it is subsequently attached to the unexpected word GAOL): we are also bringing to reading our own knowledge of the world and our own judgments. A child's 'reading age' is very much a matter of life experience and understanding, and almost never mere technique. That is why teaching computers to read is so difficult. Minsky put it thus:

Consider the following fable ...:

There was once a Wolf who saw a Lamb drinking at a river and wanted an excuse to eat it. For that purpose, even though he was himself upstream, he accused the Lamb of stirring up the water and keeping him from drinking....

To understand this, one must realize the Wolf is lying! To understand the key conjecture 'even though' one must realize that contamination never flows upstream. This in turn requires us to understand (among other things) the word 'upstream' itself.[4]

There are sub-skills involved, which can be conceptualized and listed, and some of them have been isolated and taught separately. However, this teaching is rarely meaningful on its own, and good teachers are dismissive of a reductionist 'skills' view of written language development. Where skills work is included it is part of a wider context, where the child sees reading as a sensible and rewarding activity and in which there is the chance to use reading for personally interesting purposes.[5]

In the teaching of reading (as well as its utilization) many uses of the microcomputer have been explored and proclaimed. We shall try, as usual, to examine them in their context — but remembering Bracey's question which began this chapter.

Using the Micro to Make Readers

As can be expected, the microcomputer industry has produced simple drill programs intended to reinforce and improve basic skills as they develop. Books by the end of the 1970s[6] were describing pattern recognition exercises, matching picture with word, recognizing which letters make which sound, blending three-letter trigrams, look-and-say exercises, word meanings, sorting words which were 'like' others, sentence building, timed reading followed by multiple-choice comprehension questions, and of course spelling. As we saw earlier, teachers are eager to employ game formats which give pleasure. Typically, the children will sit before the keyboard taking turns; the computer will know their names and keep a tally of their scores. It may present a word briefly, clear the screen and invite the child to type it in correctly, hoping among other things to improve retention of short-term memory; or it may present the letters jumbled up as an anagram and invite the child to work out step by step the correct answer (perhaps responding to mistakes: 'No, the first letter is B' or whatever).

It is a matter for the teacher's judgment how much use to make of these programs. A place can be argued for subskill work alongside 'holistic' approaches. The use of the microcomputer for drill can accommodate individual difference, arouse interest by a games approach, switch to different levels of difficulty and employ interest-arousing graphics. Meanwhile teachers can always intervene when necessary and develop plans for children to transfer the skills learned on the computer to the reading and writing of text.[7]

Few teachers, I suspect, would want drill to have a central role in the teaching of reading, certainly with relatively average children. But reading and writing are linked and children gain from word processing uses both for writing themselves and reading each others' efforts. The link between what a child writes and what is seen in book or on screen is more easily made when the former is regular and precise, not the wobbly scrawl of a small child's handwritten offerings. (I do not suggest abandoning handwriting entirely; writing 'on the computer' is additional, not substitute.) Earlier we quoted (page 29) the enthusiasm of Liebling for active writing on the micro using word processing; Newman[8] described a number of related activities, including a 'brainstorming' program by Steven Tschudi to help children to develop ideas on their topic by built-in 'prompts', which not only stimulated the flow of ideas but also (one suspects) enabled the children to gain a more articulate understanding of narrative content.

Many teachers claim that adventure games encourage children to think hard and work out problems, and also stimulate language use, both reading and writing. Adventure games present players with a series of situations from which they have to escape, or through which they must progress, to achieve their goal — much like some board games only in a more sophisticated form. Children usually work in groups and have to analyze the situation, hypothesize possible alternative solutions and frame their commands in appropriate terminology.[9] An American example is 'Snooper Troops'[10], a collection of mystery programs with an accompanying manual. Children collect and follow clues and have to test hypotheses, all of which are supposed to require 'reading for real purposes'.

Certainly adventure games fascinate many children, and stimulate discussion and a kind of thought; it might be worth articulating with the children (and to their parents) the skills they are developing or have developed. What is less acceptable, and worrying, is the average game's impoverished use of language, both in the program's presentation of each dilemma and (particularly) in the restricted nature of the players' responses, which are often limited to two words (for example, 'open door'). The game version of *The Hobbit* is a different experience from the original (even if for best results you have to have read the book fairly carefully). There is a danger that so far as reading skills are concerned, adventure games may be like the Blytons of yesterday, 'motivating' precisely because they do NOT stretch the child's verbal imagination or bear more than a passing resemblance to the real world or to real quests.

Nonetheless, adventure games do develop language use between children, when working in pairs or threes, and in fairness we should remember that they contain what is essentially narrative: which makes their use more 'like' extended reading than the drill exercises mentioned earlier. Moreover, the interest in sheer 'thinking skills' which de Bono has famously stimulated provides other reasons for considering adventure games, though with a similar proviso. What happens when one gets too far away from narrative-like experiences can be seen from the computer-based system described by Carver and Hoffman, giving drill to high school poor readers in 'programmed prose', pieces of writing presented and re-presented for reading and rereading until the student had demonstrated mastery: had (that is) responded correctly. While the students were working through the program, specific gains in ability were large; but sadly, afterwards the authors found there was little apparent transfer to general reading ability. The reason they felt was clear:

> ... this type of task is far removed from ordinary reading.[11]

Well, exactly. Practice in moving our arms and legs fluently does not in itself teach us to swim the Channel. It is remarkable how reluctant some teachers seem to be to get the children into the water, actually reading interesting things.

In specific cases (and especially diagnostic remedial work) artificial tasks, computer-generated or otherwise, can be helpful to the teacher, but they are insufficient and must not be relied on without other support. There are many anecdotal accounts which repay careful study. Meyer and Caldwell[12], for instance, used a variety of computer-based techniques to diagnose and help 12-year-old Martin, virtually unable to read, unresponsive to conventional remedial teaching, and reputed to have 'no memory' and to be lazy. With two specialists devoting all their time to him, using a range of computer techniques and diagnosing many of his problems (he had 'taken a dislike to activities which he perceived to be conceptual'!), very re- markable progress was made — after which he returned to school and continued exactly as before. The work, however admirable in design and intention, had not prepared him for the actual world in which he had to live — or for real reading. Yet the exercise revealed that he was perfectly capable, and that his school experiences had hindered his development, not helped it. We may comment that (pace Illich) it is unlikely that Martin would or will resolve these difficulties himself (however easily he might learn to drive a car); and that the more technology can free the teacher as well as the student from 'inauthentic labour' the more likely it is that individual guidance will be available to diagnose and treat specific difficulties, in their proper context. This is fine: but in itself, of course, it offers us no strategy on which our work could then be based. We still need the proper questions before we choose the tools that are to help with the answers. Burnett and Miller[13] gleefully described the end of a demonstration of a new computer-based reading program, when a member of the audience devastatingly but very properly asked, '*What model of reading is your program based on?*'. After an uncomfortable silence, the company representative poured out field-test results and technical detail ('our programs were designed by an internationally respected expert in' — guess what? — 'computer programming') but no answer. They commented:

> Questions about the underlying tenets of CAL programs are rare. Instead, the focus is technology. Unfortunately, many computer-based exercises in reading appear to be taken directly from basal series workbooks. The computer adds such features as graphics, automatic record-keeping, electronic page-turning and rate of presentation control.

They devized a package derived directly from current reading theory, where computer-related activities were only part of the whole, and there were no 'right' or 'wrong' answers. The student was presented successively with instalments of a story and asked to make guesses at each stage, which were later discussed. The exercise was designed to help students to see reading as a process, involving a series of approxi- mations through which we use our own language and thoughts and view of the world to build meaning. At the time of writing the package was still being field-tested, but Judith Newman[14] gave an interesting account of her own interaction with it.

This approach to reading goes directly contrary to the suggestion

by some computer enthusiasts, that reading is 'passive', a view held
(as we saw earlier) by those concentrating on what the teaching tool
did rather than what the learner was up to. Good reading reconstructs
and argues with what is being read. Now that reading specialists
are moving into the use of microcomputers themselves (rather than
criticizing the mistakes of others) we find this active, psycholinguistic view pervading the guidance they give, with children being
stimulated to 'form their own questions and interrogate the text'[15].
Teachers are urged to plan work to make students do things with
reading — unsettle the text, complete it and resequence it.[16] (Cloze
procedure, where the students must supply missing words from their
own understanding of the text's flow of meaning, is an example.)
Good project work, it is argued, require students to compare with
other texts, re-form what they found and dispute it. Thus the model
of reading from which we begin is important. Not only is reading
very much more than mere decoding of individual written shapes, it
is also considerably more complex than the checking of a number in
a telephone directory. The writer has abstracted specific elements
from the universe of experience, selecting words into sentences, and
encoding into writing; the reader decodes, perceives meaning and
patterns and reconstructs an image from the author's creation.

> It is simply impossible for any idea or information to be
> conveyed by print without both author and reader having
> thought intensively about the message.[17]

There is no reason why computer-based activities should not be
devised to help with this, as Burnett and Miller set out to do above.
The advice at the close of the Effective Use of Reading Project is
however pertinent; a programme to improve reading for learning
should include:

(a) the use of reading situations designed to foster *a willing-
     ness to reflect on what is being read*;
(b) a structure of instruction, guidance, and reading practice
     which improves the quality of reflection;
(c) arrangements to monitor methods and materials across
     the curriculum *in order to create the conditions under which
     pupils may use reading purposefully*.[18] (my emphasis)

Reflecting on what is being read is very different from the concentration of having to 'read aloud' in class or to teacher; in the latter case,
the emphasis of the poor reader is entirely on decoding words rather
than on what, if anything, they might be meaning. Poor programs

only test the very simplest of meanings, uninterestingly, like the worst kind of comprehension test. Little else is learnt, except a distaste for books. Yet skilled and confident readers can also reflect on the process of reading itself, and perhaps should be encouraged to do so. Moore[19] reviewed recent investigation into children's introspective knowledge about their own cognitive operations ('metacognition'), observing:

> Reading is undoubtedly a language-based operation requiring thinking. Given this, it would seem logical that both linguistic awareness and cognitive awareness are important factors in reading and learning to read.... In a similar way, lacking an understanding of the cognitive demands of reading could also pose problems in reading. Reading involves the interaction of reader and text.

His survey reinforced the view that poor readers 'may be ignoring relevant aspects of the reading process'. Skilled remedialists try to identify such deficient understandings and put them right. Articulating the new understandings may well help to reinforce and give confidence. As well as reflecting on what is read, readers reflect on the reading process itself, which is of course part of the 'study skills' learning emphasized in chapter 3. Perhaps the best-known of these insights is the SQ3R technique propounded in 1946 by Robinson, in which the reader is trained to survey, question, read, recite and review (see the account in Lunzer and Gardner[20]). The sharing of insight into such strategies is very different from mindless drill; it has the teacher confiding, cooperating, giving helpful advice, rather than driving the children through a seemingly meaningless succession of pointless obstacles.

The Use of Literacies

Neither reading nor 'the book' are likely to be obsolete within the foreseeable future. There may be changes in the uses made of each, and what is called 'a book' may alter its appearance; the context of other media into which reading and books fit may also change considerably. The death of reading is regularly forecast in educational revolutions (Edison's forecast about film replacing the book within ten years came in 1913) and although in some measure the still photograph, the film, sound recording, broadcasting, video and the computer all undertake tasks previously taken in less helpful ways by the printed book, publishers are today publishing more books than ever before and there seems no end to the flow. My personal suspicion is that we have not yet fully utilized the advantages of an integration of two or more of these formats, to provide what might be called 'super-books' (where the advantages of the book for extended narrative argument can be combined with moving picture and sound for additional informational enhancement) and perhaps the interactive videodisc will bring this marvel finally before us, with computer-like features in addition. It will still need to be read and understood; there is no magical 'soft option' to avoid the effort of cognition. To quote Lacy again, the concept of an accumulation of knowledge being termed a 'database' reveals:

> the assumption that important knowledge consists of an accumulation of discrete facts ... that the needs and mode of thought of an inquirer are ... not those of someone who reads a novel or a biography or a poem. And the oft-expressed conviction that the computer will make the book obsolete reveals a perhaps unconscious but arid and constricted belief regarding the nature of important knowledge and important communication.[21]

The further one progresses into almost any subject area, the more one discovers difficulty, unfamiliar concepts, contention, differences of opinion or interpretation, variations in approach and competing schools of thought, all of which require the linear analysis and extended discussion of the kind journal articles and books are well suited (one is tempted to say uniquely suited) to provide. Scientific TV programmes and magazines, for instance, revel in debate which books further explicate: and social sciences, not to mention the notoriously anarchic arts and humanities, are battlegrounds of competing realities, and properly so. Not only is it important for students to be ready to deal with such dissension and discussion, often arguable at considerable length, but the realities of human experience are themselves only expressible in discursive and extended form, in (among other formats) printed accounts. There is every reason therefore why any sensible education system should aim as rapidly as possible at introducing students to 'reading at length and in depth'. This is how a great deal of what is important in adult life will always have to be accessed; and just as importantly, the very act of regular reading is itself the best possible practice of the skills it requires. As Frank Smith never tires of saying, we 'learn to read by reading'.[22]

How much of such reading happens in our schools? Lunzer

and Gardner, to their consternation, found very little reading of an extended nature. Projects which require only a minimum of reading (perhaps three sentences) from a minima of sources (one reference book) hardly meet that necessary concern. Moreover, to postpone any really detailed comparison of lengthy texts until the sixth form (16–19), with all its examination pressures and the inauthentic activity which the University of East Anglia study revealed[24] leaves those who never reach that far wholly unprepared and those who do inadequately helped. A restructured curriculum seeking a balance between content and skills must be developed if (as most teachers, reports suggest) sufficient attention to crucial literacy is difficult under the present system. The movement for 'Reading Across the Curriculum' can, at best, claim only a limited success and the subsequent concern over 'study skills' may well run itself into the ground if it becomes associated only with the mechanical application of unconsidered rules and procedures. One remembers how 'library skills' used to be taught, by teacher-librarians or during the English lessons (or both): an ill-informed explanation of the 'ten categories' of the Dewey Decimal Classification, a look at the (usually incompetent) school library catalogue, a trot round shelves and a word or two about indexes, alphabetical order and noting down references: none of it meaningful to the students because none of it linked with what happened elsewhere, nor arising during a teaching/learning context when any of the skills mentioned were particularly important.

J.G. Ballard once criticized pulp science fiction as consisting of 'unearned experience'. It is not only writers of computer programs to teach supposed reading skills who show a similar fault. Lunzer and Gardner's team studying the use of books and reading in a large number of classrooms found not just that little reading was ever done but that teachers held what can best be described as uninformed notions of the use of text and the nature of the act of reading. And yet what is literacy if it does not enable its possessor to expect and cope with uncertainty and a variety of opinions and options? And how far is this helped by less than one minute's scanning of one easily located text and what educational use is a question satisfied by such scanty and trivial research?

Knowledge is more than merely knowing, and includes active reprocessing skills:

> ... the ability to use deductive and inductive reasoning including the scientific method, the ability to read and process information (which includes application, analysis, synthesis

and evaluation skills) and the ability to transmit information via print and telecommunications. This constitutes literacy in its general and scientific sense.[24]

Such teaching best takes place when the teacher has personally and consciously explored, in some depth, the experience of reading for meaning and of 'the use of knowing' which is its context, and has been helped to translate that experience into an understanding of the developmental nurturing of these skills among students — whatever subject area the teacher may otherwise claim as a specialism. It is no criticism of teachers in their present beleaguered plight to say that such a translation has not always been complete. When your most typical and repetitive reading activity is marking workbooks, perhaps your view of reading is bound to be unconsciously limited.

The place of wide recreational reading in the student's (and perhaps one dare add the teacher's) educational development has been constantly emphasized in the literature of English teaching and that of school librarianship. However, education is bedevilled by the existence of parallel literatures that never meet at any point. One wonders how many teachers of other subjects have read them. If the skill of reading involves the interaction of the reader with the text, then the more closely the reader is 'pulled into' the text by interest (what the jargon calls 'the affective mode') and the more practice the reader has of interacting with a wide range of such texts the better. Good learners (not simply good readers) tend to be those who came into contact with books and stories at home before they even began school, as the Bristol Language Development Project is currently rediscovering[25] and much of this is attributable to their grasp of the different uses of language between what is spoken and what is written. (As the parents can hardly be assumed to have consciously set out to 'teach' this, presumably the children learnt by 'discovery'.) Few secondary teachers other than those associated with the English department see it as their responsibility to take active steps to encourage voluntary pleasurable reading (which need not always be of fiction), perhaps partly because one can rarely expect to see an immediately testable result from it. Yet the teacher of geography, history or science (say) who is seen by students to be a keen reader and who from time to time shares subject enthusiasm through recommended casual reading (and makes sure such books are in the school library collection) is playing a major part in carrying out the wider educational aims of almost any school.

Just as non-reading children are made by non-reading parents, so the issue is compounded by non-reading teachers.[26] But it is not just a lack of obvious enthusiasm for reading that indicates the teacher whose pupils are at risk. 'Unearned experience' means that it is common to find very enthusiastic teachers, anxious to employ the project method and encourage pupil autonomy, who nonetheless show insufficient personal understanding of the process to carry this properly through. This is where it is so sad that the 'parallel literatures' syndrome operates, and that teachers do not normally read the journal articles and books primarily intended for school librarians — just as (say) English teachers rarely read articles on projects in geography or social studies which might be of relevance to them.

The Importance of Depth

What is 'reading'? Much classroom practice would suggest, as Lunzer and Gardner found, that it is scanning a sentence or so from a book, reproducing it in one's 'topic', and nothing more. Chambers commented:

> I fear it is not uncommon for children to be encouraged to gather in this undiscriminating manner bits and pieces from every kind of book. What betrays this approach is that children are thus misled as to the true nature and value of literature, treating it as a resource in the educationally technical sense of that trendy word, rather than as an experience to be entered into, shared and contemplated. It is the difference between 'using' and 'sharing' literature.[27]

We need not limit this to literature; other media, and life itself, are subject to the 'Autolycus approach', the gathering up of unconsidered trifles. Project work to be successful must avoid this trap, and as students at all levels (including higher education) know, it is all too easy to impress teacher by the range of one's snippet-gathering (proving one's 'information skills', using catalogues and tools, collecting a convincing mass of data) without the exercise having amounted to anything more meaningful. Yes, there are occasions when, and pupils for whom, to have done so much is an acceptable step forward, but it is a small part of the journey, not the destination. All the enquiry, the seeking out of sources and the comparing of data amount to very little if there is not an incentive to 'reflect on what is being read', and to make from it not just a project report but also meaning.

This includes the opportunity not only to find and think but also to feel and empathize. James Britton[28] spoke of the real danger of 'imposing a disjunction between thought and feeling, between cognitive and affective modes of representation', and he went on to emphasize 'the value and importance both of the discursive logical organization and at the same time that of the undissociated intuitive processes, the organization represented in its highest form in works of art'.

The newer arts, like film, and the running discourse of popular music, will be examined in the next section. But although modern teenagers are reputed not to read, there is massive publication and reading of a kind. Literature remains one of the most effective ways in which human beings communicate and Richard Hoggart's words are relevant here:

> I value literature because of the way — the peculiar way — in which it explores, re-creates and seeks for the meanings in human experience; because it explores the diversity, complexity and strangeness of that experience (of individual men, of men in groups or of men in relation to the natural world); because it re-creates the texture of that experience; and because it pursues its explorations with disinterested passion ... I value literature because in it men look at life with all the vulnerability, honesty, and penetration they can command.[29]

Young people read comic books, paperback romances and thrillers, semi-pornographic magazines and lengthy semi-fictional accounts of their favourite pop idols — as well as viewing films, TV soap operas and much else of that kind. If many teenagers do not respond easily to the literature with which school presents them, there may be at least two out of many other factors operating: they may not have been led to view pleasurable reading as an ordinary and essential part of life, from primary school upwards, and they may be experiencing culture-clash as they establish their own identities in contradistinction to our own. Equally, of course, being honest can be painful, and adolescence is often painful enough on its own without the addition of unemployment, cuts in education and social security, and the threat of nuclear annihilation. Whatever the cause, treating literature as a 'resource for snippets' is unlikely to help. There must be occasions when 'reading at length and in depth', and responding with emotion and commitment, is not only natural but required.

Sherry Turkle[30] related this factor to video games and computers, noting that 'young people are building their generation's culture now' and that such elements were among the materials of that culture.

> Growing up with a technology is a special kind of experi-
> ence.... The games are not a reminder of a feeling of control
> over challenge. They are a primary source for developing it.

She found young people whose emotional involvement with games of the dungeons and dragons variety was profound. Such games are not trivial; thick rule books make clear the structure of the imaginary universe they present and the constraints on decision-making at each stage. Of one of her subjects, Jarish, she wrote:

> After reading seven dungeons and dragons books 'about
> twenty times' he certainly knows more about the structure of
> dungeon universes than he does about any moment in history.
> He knows more about the behavior of magic users than about
> any person who ever lived. What he learns in social studies
> classes about real history is pale in contrast to his experiences
> in D and D. 'I mean', says Jarish, 'in D and D there is so much
> data'.

The challenge to educators is clearly to make the world we present to the Jarishes in our class as real and vivid as the fantasy universes (whether in D and D, soap operas, or pop culture) to which they retreat. In this particular instance it may mean beginning with science fiction, whose emotional and imaginative range has dramatically widened in recent years, but whatever the approach the requirement of time for reflection and for prolonged study of the material is paramount. Chambers again:

> A reader who is never challenged, unsettled or moved, who
> has never realized how books can be — intentionally or
> otherwise — subversive, is a reader who does not know. He
> does not know how to receive literature, does not know how
> to discover his responses or how to express himself to
> others.[31]

It is a characteristic of the 'shallow response' to the computer information world to think in terms of using the technology to find the answers. But answers are not always to be found, and it is only through lengthy study and encouraged reflection that many of us begin to reconsider our questions and look more deeply for their resolution. This is not an activity which is promoted either by the 'instructional unit' approach of direct teaching and CAL, or by the fact-hunting versions of the group or individual project.

The Other Literacies

Literacy, knowing how to read and write, is accepted as essential to the educated person. Numeracy, or basic mathematical under-standing, traditionally goes alongside as its partner, and has been receiving (very properly) increased emphasis in official reports and sometimes in practice. By analogy, teachers and others have begun to emphasize what are described as other 'literacies', and many of them will have been implicit in the analysis in earlier chapters: 'computer literacy', 'visual literacy', 'media literacy' and so on. Some enthusiasts in the 'informations skills' movement have even invented the word 'informacy' to express what they see as an important new area of concern.

Purists will bridle at what seems an improper use of the term: 'literacy' derives from the Latin word for 'letters', and what does that have to do with computers or audio-visual media? That is a side-issue, although some implications will be examined at the appropriate stage of discussion. The present book is centrally concerned with skills and the recognition of their place in curriculum, and we shall accept as a starting point the definition of literacy given by Ruthven:

> a progression through which an individual acquires increasing familiarity with, and mastery of, a set of interwoven strands of knowledge and skill.[32]

That description certainly fits reading and writing; what other 'literacies' should schools now consider?

'Computer Literacy' in a World of Change

Speakers at educational conferences often assert that today's students must be 'literate, numerate and computerate' — and while the purists again writhe at the terminology other critics will be ready to point out apparent logical flaws. As Suhor[33] commented, people in 1900 who were alert to the trends of the times could have argued for 'auto literacy', on the grounds that motor cars were certainly going to transform our society in astonishing ways. Equally, at around the same time, futurologists could have argued that the invention of the telephone was going to make schools obsolete. In fact, education literature shows no trace of these arguments, and even if people had been far-sighted enough to consider them would they have been justified? A student commented waspishly that on such analogies we might be putting on 'pop-up toaster awareness courses'.

However, whereas the pop-up toaster merely replaced the fire and the toasting fork with a convenient alternative that didn't need watching, the computer has given us a machine which totally transforms what we can do, what we can conceive of doing, and how we think about information itself. The novelty is not the point; the transformation is.

Thus computer education, of some sort, is a very different case and it was not surprising to find 'computer literacy' being defined officially in the USA by the *Journal of Reading* in these terms:

> We are computer literate when we are able (1) to control the computer and program it in some computer language, (2) use prepared programs and judge their qualities, and (3) pass on these skills to other people.[34]

This definition is clearly aimed at teachers, and teacher-readers may at this point like to examine their own competence to see whether they are up to scratch. More importantly, is it an accurate description of what all schoolchildren should reasonably be expected to master during schooling?

Here we may try analogies to see whether they help. A description of 'musical literacy' might include, as well as elements of musical 'appreciation', the ability to play an instrument and to both read and write music in some recognized form of musical notation. Vast numbers of people listen to music of one kind or another, go to concerts and festivals, watch films and television programmes where music plays an important part, and sing in pubs, football stadiums and the bath. What should we be required to teach in schools?

Now return to 'auto literacy': an important part of driving instruction used to be how to change gear. Once it was a skilled and delicate operation: later with technical improvement one could change from fourth to first in one step without trouble; today a large number of cars are on automatic drive. Meanwhile the UK is one of few countries which offer a driving licence to people who have not been tested in the maintenance of their engines.

I offer no opinion on these analogies but they can help our thinking about what we need to teach about computers. The three 'paradigms' to follow are based loosely on the helpful analysis by Ruthven[35] though with my own expansion and examples.

> *We could concentrate on teaching technique: students would learn how a computer works, and the technical skills of operating it.*

This would include a look at the inner parts of the computer, the mysteries of the microchip, the binary logic on which it works, the use of a computer with specific pieces of software, and an introduction to one or other of the current computer languages.

The difficulty with this paradigm is not so much that it is misleading or contains unnecessary elements, but that computers change and so do their users. Some MSC courses have been on this pattern but how relevant will they be in a few years' time with different generations of computers? The courses are restricted in scope, and may easily become marginalized unless great efforts are made to integrate such work with the rest of the curriculum. Their main virtue is that they do lead to a (temporary) 'mastery of technique' — which may soon become obsolete.

> *Students are helped to develop an awareness of computer technology in its social and economic context.*

Some new 16+ courses are of this kind and certainly students can helpfully examine the role and social effects of the new technology as a result, so far as can at present be judged. Once again however their characteristics are specific to the current state of the art, and there is a much smaller element of 'technique mastery', for good or ill.

A Minnesota project on these lines included (with typical transatlantic thoroughness) no less than fifty cognitive objectives and nine affective objectives. Among the latter (and this is typical of many such courses in our own country) was the development of 'positive attitudes towards computers'. One may wonder whether this is a proper educational objective ('Love your machine-loom'), and whether one would be required to fail a student who completed the course honestly concluding, for clearly elaborated reasons, that the balance of the evidence was negative?

> *Students are given access to tools, and the ability to use computers as tools. They learn to recognize situations where computers are appropriate, and to select, design and implement solutions.*

This reminds us of Papert's view of the computer as 'an object to think with'. Ruthven's hope was that such work would be appropriate in every area of the curriculum. What he was less sure of, and it may be important for us to find out, was whether problem-solving in one area taught skills that carried over into other subjects. Papert's LOGO, after all, takes place in a wider context of activities.

> Many interactive packages require users to frame appropriate questions and commands, and to interpret and respond appropriately to the statements, instructions and questions which the system generates in response.[36]

It remains to be seen how much 'the system' constrains the acquisition of full understanding without cross-curricular intervention. This paradigm requires more careful planning than the other two, indeed demands a 'whole-school policy' which might sensibly be linked to that for other information-using skills. On the other hand it has the advantage of giving opportunity for the generation of insight rather than the training of limited but specific competence.

Whichever paradigm we prefer, there are problems. The great danger with the first two is that the separation of the computer course to another and distinct part of the timetable may mean that students do not see it as relevant to their own personal interests and quests. The equal danger of paradigm three is that, by dispersing the subject matter across the school it may get lost. Only those things will be taught and learnt which happen to suit the style and pattern of each subject teacher. We have still not stated (readers will have noted) WHAT we think it important for the whole-school policy to contain.

We will look at some specific candidates for inclusion in a moment. Meanwhile we should look at another alternative which Ruthven offered, and which has been in the air in a rather diffuse state for some time, often arising from other starting points but leading to a similar conclusion. This is the suggestion of a much larger curricular unit which would include and absorb what we have so far discussed but place it in a different whole. Ruthven suggested 'The development of technological literacy'. The advantage he saw was that such a unit was too large for one specific department (for example, science) to mount entirely on its own but would depend upon inter-departmental co-operation. He suggested five components: mechanisms; techniques; functions; applications; social context and implications.

It is always stimulating to take a new look at curriculum groupings, and there is an interesting logic about this particular proposal that might well commend itself particularly to those concerned about our industrial and technological survival. The difficulty I see, which could well be overcome if the new large unit was accompanied by others equally well planned, is that the information-using components might tend to get separated from their fellows in the non-technological area. Many of the uses of computers, we have seen, were related to thinking and finding out and transforming, activities which happen across the curriculum and not located in only one unit, however major. Nonetheless, we shall examine this model again at a later stage of the chapter.

Programming and 'Languages'

There are two ways in which we use a computer. One involves locating the appropriate piece of software which then enables us to do what we want with the machine. The other is to write that software for ourselves. Hackers and computer hobbyists scorn the first and insist on the second; some teachers have laboriously taught themselves to program simply because the quality of much available software is so low. The vast majority of computer users in industry, commerce, the public sector and the home market operate computers to their relative satisfaction on the basis of programs bought off the peg or written for them by highly-trained specialists.

This does not mean that there is no point in learning programming: it does mean that the purpose of learning it is not 'in order to be able to use a computer'. Why might an adult wish to understand programming?

1   To be able to understand something of how computers work.
2   To be able to discuss with, and give instructions to, professional programmers who are designing to one's own specifications.
3   To be able to amend and adapt other people's programs to fit more closely specific personal needs.
4   For pleasure — the same sort of discipline that comes from making things or solving logical puzzles.
5   To be able to work as a professional programmer oneself.

So far as schoolchildren are concerned, it is likely that only a small proportion will have the talent and temperament to succeed as computer professionals, and programming courses at school are by no means a royal road to success in the field. Indeed, school 'computer science courses' are despised by many course-tutors for computing degrees, and by many managers of computer businesses; all too often, children have been taught bad programming habits by semi-skilled teachers and have virtually to start again from square one.

There remain the other reasons, of which the first is by far the most important. To know something of how a program is constructed and how a computer responds gives insight not only into the workings of the machine but also into its limitations, what it is not good at. No-one can wrestle with programming for long without being struck, not only by the beauty of a well-constructed program but also by the blinkered stupidity of what at first seems to be an intelligent mechanism: its inability to recognize patterns, to make intuitive leaps, to make its own connections. When a child says, 'Of course, the computer doesn't know that because I haven't told it yet' an important fact has been grasped and demystification begun.

Computer studies courses at present tend to include largeish chunks of programming by BASIC, the equivalent in computing of the Dewey Decimal Classification in libraries — widely deplored and almost universally used. There is a significant movement among computing teachers to emphasize other languages (LOGO, Pascal, PROLOG or COMAL) and to decry BASIC for teaching harmful programming practices that give no real insight into how computers actually work. Atherton has been particularly harsh[37] but not alone. As a total non-specialist who has worked away personally at BASIC like most home computer owners, I find the arguments very persuasive, the only question being what one does about them.

LOGO[38] has two clear advantages: first, it is a valuable tool for mathematical understanding; and second, it enables the pupil to instruct the machine rather than the other way round. The youngest child using LOGO is successfully pushing the turtle around almost from Go. As an introduction to how computers operate, LOGO is also excellent; and non-mathematical uses are now being explored (for instance, LOGO music). A possible disadvantage is that LOGO takes up a large area of computer memory; this may be less of a problem as machines themselves develop. Any subject which involves, for instance, the manipulation of shapes (and several come to mind) can use LOGO with benefit. Where, however, the proposed uses are verbal, we appear to have less evidence as yet.

Pascal, on the other hand, in many ways a well-structured language which Atherton for one has praised, may pose problems for students of only modest attainment.[39] It has been traditionally implemented as a 'compiler', that is, it requires separate editing and translation steps, in contrast to the immediacy of BASIC or LOGO.

Apart from COMAL, there is a growing lobby for PROLOG which is publicized as in accord with 'Fifth Generation' Japanese developments, based on logical procedures that are not narrowly mathematical.[40] We are in the hands of the specialists and await their creative response. Already there are programs to produce programs, and it may well be that present ways of communicating with and programming a microcomputer will become increasingly obsolete. Meanwhile there seems no sensible reason why all children should be drilled through a system of instruction-giving like BASIC ('could cause health hazards on a scale that makes anthrax seem like the common cold', said someone) which serves no other purpose for them.

Some writers compare such languages with human languages. This is improper, in that with human languages one is also getting into some sort of touch with the lives and feelings of people. As one teacher put it:

> It assumes that language no longer emanates from the life of a community, from geographical place, from heritage, ritual, from the living body of a people, from the voice of things in the world. . . .[41]

He went on to describe computer terminology as 'the enslaving of language', a jaundiced view. But those who, in praise of the strict rationality and linear nature of a programming language, compare it for its disciplinary value with the learning of Latin, have clearly never encountered the beauty of Virgil and Ovid or contemplated the possibility of doing so. The main purpose of learning a programming language, when one is ready to do so, is in order to accomplish one's own goals and objectives. Students in schools should be enabled to do this, in as many areas of the curriculum as can be accommodating. Some students will wish to go further, and explore in greater depth, and should be able to do so. All students should at some stage make computers do simple things of their own choice, for the sake of the understanding the experience will bring: and it is up to educators, and the designers of systems friendly to education, to make these occasions meaningful.

Media Literacy

At this point we may pause and look at further examples of communication technology. The computer is only one of the latest (at the time of writing, the interactive videodisc is the very latest) and there have been successive revolutions ever since the invention of photography, which for the first time gave us the concept (deceitful as it turned out) of a purely objective record. We spend many hours of the average teaching week educating pupils to find meaning correctly out of printed verbal record (in most subject areas) and very properly; much less time is spent on ensuring that they learn how to 'read' visual images, get an appropriate message from what they see, and stay on guard against manipulation in any format.

Yet there must be many teachers who have considered the contrast, and who would have some sympathy with an American colleague's complaint that schools spend twelve years trying to produce critical readers (though the average American adult reads one book a year) and do nothing about TV, despite statistics of four to six hours viewing daily for life.[42]

He urged that new information technology (of all kinds) be incorporated into our classroom activities in ways that 'suit *our* goals for *our*selves and *our* students'. (his emphasis)

It may be that a critical attitude, once developed towards reading, may transfer to other areas and formats, though I know of no actual evidence here. Ruth argued that there need be no conflict between print and non-print, and that we needed:

> a broader based literacy that develops skills of investigation and interpretation, that must include both verbal and visual 'texts'.[43]

Ferguson has argued that media studies offered an activity concerned with the construction of meaning, and that:

> The development of language skills parallel with a cognitive awareness of the functioning of media is probably the most important aspect of practical work in media studies.[44]

Narrative is narrative, however and wherever it shows itself. Understanding how it works in cinema may help our appreciation of how it works in a written text. One brand of current literary criticism includes this assumption; it is due to arrive in our schools.

In an earlier chapter (page 38) we saw that interpreting biological evidence required regular practice as well as teaching. The process of deciding what we are actually observing is learned; it is a cognitive act which depends on a set of developed assumptions. I nod my head and you are encouraged: but in some cultures the gesture means 'No'. Go round an exhibition, of an artist or subject matter unfamiliar to you; then go round again listening to commentary from the artist or exhibition organizer on tape; what you see will change. Richard Kool[45] usefully analyzed the process of 'reading' objects in a museum. Because seeing is active, he was able to distinguish three steps: ISOLATE (where one concentrates on what is to be examined, without distraction or irrelevant context); INSPECT (where the item is actually studied); and INSERT (where the inspected item is 'placed' in a conceptual structure or mental background). To do this properly we may have to do some research; some techniques were specific to particular periods or peoples, and some symbols are very culture-specific.

This is a comparable process to the examination of poetry; we study the meanings of words at the time identified ('naughty' is not what it was) and the imagery related to ideas and beliefs then current, and as a result arrive at 'the poem' as distinct from an imprecise vision of it. The process by which we examine a major religious painting closely resembles how we might examine a newspaper advertisement or a television news report. Here is a painting of a mother and child; we recognize a Nativity, but why is there a lamb and other animals, and various unexpected objects, and what do they mean? We learn that they are symbols expressing what the painter is trying (or required) to say about the 'meaning' of the scene. Now we see an advertisement for a brand of tinned soup: why is the soup served in elegant surroundings, gleaming tablecloth, expensive silverware and glass, glamorous couple in dinner jacket and dazzling dress, confident loving smiles . . .? What is the advertiser trying to tell us about tinned soup — and what difference does it make when we notice? In the television news report: what symbols accompany the words? What is the effect of contrast? — for instance, angry pickets in scruffy outdoor clothes saying incoherent things to camera, followed by smiling well-dressed management giving calm statistical evidence for the justice of their response from behind a tidy desk. And would it affect us if the boss had a five-o'clock shadow?

Sometimes this analytical exercise is called 'visual literacy', and again there are those who cavill at the term. Cassidy and Knowlton[46] saw it as a 'failed metaphor', and one can see that a really close comparison between the 'grammar' of reading a text and the shifting imprecision of 'reading the visual image' may not be possible. This does not mean that a study of how information 'presents' in different formats is not worth while: only that we might be careful what we call it. Contrasts of angles, lighting, close-up or long-shot, confident wave or fascist-like salute can be chosen and manipulated to have their effect, and if we are guided to perceive them we are less likely to respond unintelligently. Those who attempt to mould our responses improperly may therefore be less successful; and those who respond unthinkingly to what they see may be guided to get a more truthful impression and to lead a more considered life.

All over the UK, schoolchildren contributed to the BBC Domesday Project, taking surveys and photographs of their localities for the purpose of a permanent videodisc archive. One hopes they received good advice on the effects of camera angle and how to choose what each frame would actually show. How would each picture be described, and indeed, what is a still photograph 'about'? The BBC Film Library once indexed a film clip of a Trafalgar Square demonstration under every heading they could imagine, only to find that for one visitor it was memorable for showing an unusually rare type of pigeon. Captions make a difference: a Third World figure with a gun, smiling or not, is perceived differently if captioned FREEDOM FIGHTER from when captioned TERRORIST. What we 'see' is based on our mental constructs.

So just as we examine the contrasting imagery of Cleopatra's dying speech and the interjections of her maid, so we can examine the contrasting imagery of persuasion and presentation in the visual formats. Such studies make us more critically aware of the information saturation in which we live, and help us to develop deeper understanding of our own perceptions. Of course, Shakespeare is safely 'historical' and the problems he dealt with distanced by time (we do not need to care so deeply about the historical truth of his Richard III); looking at images from our own time brings us closer to the investigation of present power structures and questions not always convenient to special interest groups. Sometimes this has gathered the label 'political' — as if not to mention them was not political! — but we dare not settle for training children for conformity. We are educating for a world of change, and they will need an attitude of enquiring scepticism, backed up by such understanding of human values as we can properly develop. When pressurized by business interests, unions, or politicians of right, centre or left, the profession should stand firm. It is wholly improper that we accept interference on major issues.

Then what is 'media literacy'? As with reading, and computer understanding, it cannot be separated from doing: writing, and handling a camera or tape recorder, trimming a picture to make it tell your story, understanding map conventions, making two- or three-dimensional diagrams, constructing models. It is based on critical and sensitive analysis: not only of what is present but sometimes on what is not. I suggested five questions which might be asked of any pictorial representation[47] and these can be more widely applied:

1   What's there in the picture? (analysis of detail).
2   How do we know what is there? (the picture as evidence).
3   What is also there? (detail we may be ignoring).
4   What isn't there? (this may be just as revealing).
5   What is the picture 'saying'? (and is it true?).

For this picture, where must the cameraperson have been standing? What was happening out of shot? What should happen if we saw it with a different lens, in long shot not close up, or in wide angle? An analysis of the sensitive use of imagery in movies helps our understanding of the development of narrative and how imagery propels it: one long scene is shot in oppressively confined surroundings, we are very aware of walls and ceilings and spatial constraints: then suddenly the scene explodes outside, horses riding furiously off across the enormous prairie under the huge sky. Or how women are visually treated in the movie (even which types of women are chosen to appear) can tell us a great deal about the 'hidden curriculum' of the story.

Thus most of 'media literacy' is the thinking that lies behind perception. Seeing is a cognitive act and we are training mental alertness just as much as in peering down microscopes, the observation on a geography field trip or in geometric analysis. It is worth noting that we are not concerned, as perhaps we might have thought we should be twenty years ago, with teaching children to load cameras and tape recorders and switch machines off and on. They know all this for themselves and if not it is not very difficult or interesting. So far as machine use is concerned, what we emphasize is the sensitive and intelligent deployment of creative facilities for their purposes, for (as Ferguson said) the creation of meaning. The reception element in any information-processing format is the least interesting and problematic.

This is not a matter which can be safely left to English and social studies teachers. Geography teachers are not only looking at visual images in maps and charts, but also at photographic data which needs decoding. Some of it — rocks, landscapes, weather patterns — may be straightforward visual analysis; but other examples, especially in human geography, will carry secondary as well as primary messages and the good teacher will be alert for unintended racism or sexism, as well as for unthinking responses such as touristy quaintness. In both geology and archaeology, we are looking at 'frozen time', or time made space, with vivid imaginative potential. In history we look at artefacts, pictures and old documents analytically in ways that teach us to separate strangeness and commonness, and also to view our own times in a novel way. Modern language teaching has its part to play here too, in the sensitive exploration of another culture not only through words but through typical visual perceptions.

Whether the word 'literacy' is entirely accurate for such developed perceptions is no doubt debated but the arguments are sterile. No-one in whom such understanding has not been aroused is either fully educated or, in a world saturated with images, wholly 'free'. On any occasion when curriculum is rethought (today would be a good moment!) we must bring out for reexamination the question of the perception of information, in all its forms. If we are moving into the 'new information society', then our students need to be ready for active use of all the forms in which information is presented. To limit ourselves to the reading of words and their manipulation on computers is, in a media-rich society, a remarkable truncation of the possible.

Media, Computers and the Information Curriculum

We are now in a position to draw conclusions from the argument of this chapter, and to relate them to the major argument of the book. We saw earlier that Ruthven proposed a large curriculum unit on 'the development of technological literacy', and those of us who believe that technology (as the application of human knowledge to the solution of human problems) has been seriously undervalued in British education will feel sympathetic to the idea. Students who choose to give their studies an increasingly technological orientation (and the ability to do this should obviously be available in the later years of secondary schooling) will find such a programme beneficial, and in a modified form others should have exposure to it.

Nonetheless, such a programme on its own (and to be fair, Ruthven made no such limiting suggestion) would be in great danger of neglecting the fundamental information studies component we have been exploring, and which is the underlying foundation of both technological and non-technological study. One 'use of knowing' is that we can change our world (which is what technology is about), but once we begin asking 'in what way?' and 'for what purposes?' we are out of 'the development of technological literacy' and into social and humane studies. In all three areas we need to explore the ways in which we know including the important component of 'shared knowledge' on which our society rests: an understanding of the richly varied ways in which human knowledge presents itself to us in the 'new information society', together with the recognition that this is in an important sense a precious gift which we inherit and to which we may be (in some way we shall need to think out) 'responsible'.

Newton said that if he saw further than some it was because he 'stood on the shoulders of giants'. Eliot defined living in the present as living 'in the present moment of the past'. Without a sense of the changing and developing nature of human knowledge, we shall be unprepared for what we find, and if we examine what we find only in the context of technology we shall miss other dimensions. This makes it imperative not to locate information studies, or particular aspects of them, in one sectional curriculum area. In modern circumstances it would be absurd to limit studies of the computer (say) to mathematics and science, of the book to literature and history, and audiovisual media to the social sciences. The study of how information presents is usefully and essentially interdisciplinary.

Those teachers tending to concentrate more and more on skills acquired in process can meet together at this juncture. We have tended to work away in our own areas with our own preconceptions and our own 'parallel literatures': writing skills, reading skills, language skills, communication skills, study skills, library skills, number skills, computer skills, media skills, enquiry skills, research skills, creative skills, thinking skills. . . . If we return to the question I asked teachers in 1970, 'What is a resource?', we remember that the answer was all-embracing and comprehensive: 'Anything which can be an object of study or stimulus to the student' (which necessarily included items that were especially 'an aid to the teacher').[48] The study of individual subject disciplines is the basis for the study of what pervades them all: the ways in which we conceptualize, communicate, manipulate, understand and in the meantime store what we know.

The detail of what we know changes (as we saw with 'continental drift' and 'plate tectonics') but although the ways in which we know steadily multiply and their interrelationships change, there is a general continuity which makes it the single most valuable general product of an education system. In this sense, we can insist that education is not about 'knowing' but 'the use of knowing'. 'Subjects' are means, not ends. The 'autonomous learner' is not the one who knows the jigsaw pattern of concepts in different subjects but who knows the under-lying skills by which these concepts are arrived at and can be used for further understanding.

The Network-Skills for Understanding

The skills we have identified at various points so far interrelate as a network foundation to curriculum.

1 *Language and reading skills.* Whatever the experiences necessary to the understanding of individual subjects, language is the major tool for articulating that understanding, and reading a major form in which language is presented. Thus we detected the following abilities:
   — to define and communicate need through language;
   — to recognize and understand such communications from others;
   — to use language, including written language, as a tool for the formation and consideration of concepts;
   — to search written texts for specific pieces of information;
   — to learn through longer study of written texts, in ways that could then be restated in the student's own terms or formats;
   — to understand and respond to creative and imaginative uses of written language as well as factual and theoretical accounts;
   — to recognise limitations of language, including occasions of bias, restrictions of language codes and theoretical structures, and the 'indescribable and unsayable'.

2 *Number skills*: not merely the mechanical manipulation of number but developing mathematical understanding and the ability to construct and use mathematical reasoning and analysis for the solution of problems. These will include (and others better qualified will be able to add more):
   — the perception of numerical and spatial relationships;
   — the use of mathematical analysis to reveal pattern and meaning, and to validate or invalidate intuitive guesses.

3 *Observational skills*, recognizing that 'to see' is a cognitive skill, requiring active questioning of detail and the construction of pattern. Thus the abilities involved include:
   — the nature of 'observation' in the different disciplines (for example, how would a botanist, a geographer and an artist 'observe' a patch of woodland?);
   — the techniques of recording observation in different disciplines.

4 *Use of tools and sources*, especially those concerned with communication and information storage. These include:

— written sources (books, journals, indexing tools) as in 1 above;

— audio-visual sources (sound recordings, still and moving visuals, studied or made), where the skills will link with 3 above;

— computer sources, including accessing and responding to programs already prepared, and using the computer to create programs to respond to need. Some of this will link with 1 above, other aspects with 2 and 3;

— collected sources and organizations of information, including libraries and resource centres, museums and galleries, advice units and online computer databanks. All three of the above sections will be relevant here;

— laboratories, workshops, 'the real world', where the skills of hypothesising, experimenting and analyzing will call particularly on 1 and 2, and also on the kind of thinking skills necessary for 3.

5 *Manual and physical skills*, including the use of equipment and implements for the carrying out of physical tasks, the manufacture of objects or constructions, and the expressive use of the body (as in painting and dance). The use of information materials in conjunction with (say) metalwork equipment or a pottery wheel reminds us again of the interrelationships between different kinds of skill in today's society.

This list is partial and specialists will be able to fill in details I have not taken the trouble to think out. Language use for instance brings us to foreign languages, including those spoken by important groups of people in our own country. The criticism some of us would make of the lists of 'skills curricula' common in some American school districts is that the lists are partial, typically drawn up by library media specialists with a correspondingly blinkered range. No doubt chasing after interrelationships and networks can turn into the theorist's equivalent of 'spaghetti programs' in BASIC computing. However there is a sense in which the library media centre offers a useful paradigm on which a skills program for wider purposes can be constructed. The library media centre contains printed, audio-visual and computer resources: it calls upon print literacy, visual and aural literacy, and computer literacy, and one can imagine asking 'questions' of the real world in a similar sense to the way one 'questions' a library — formulating first what one wishes to find out, deciding where in the location chosen the 'answer' is likely to be, and in what way it is likely to manifest itself. The main difference between the library and the 'real world' is that the latter has not already been classified for us by somebody else in an overt way. And that need not be much of a disadvantage!

The Literacies in a Whole-School Policy

We return to our major theme: what is it important to know about 'the use of knowing'? Our discussion so far has ranged over teaching methodologies, among information sources, in and out of information skills and across a number of types of equipment. It may be useful to take stock of the messages we are trying to convey to the students in our care.

1 Education is a quest for personal meaning. The courses and classes are there to help towards that meaning: they don't themselves provide it.
2 A major purpose of instruction is to lead the student nearer to independence and the ability to learn for oneself.
3 The world of knowledge is enormous and always increasing. It is impossible to know everything but possible to find out what one needs from what is known.
4 Knowing is a personal construct from the interaction of information and experience. Education can help with the routes towards that information and provide beneficial experiences but meaning is what one makes of it in the process.
5 Learning is therefore a skill, or rather a set of skills. You learn these skills in the process of exploring content, but they are more lasting and valuable because the content element may change with time.

Notes

1. BRACEY, G.W. (1982) 'Computers in education: What the research shows', *Electronic Learning*, 2, 3, November/December, pp. 51–4
2. LACY, D. (1983) 'Reading in an audiovisual and electronic era', *Daedalus*, 112, 1, winter, pp. 117–27.
3. FREIRE, P. (1984) 'World within world: A critical reading of the universe', *Unesco Courier*, February, pp. 29–31.

4. MINSKY, M. (1975) 'A framework for representing knowledge', WINSTON, P.H. (Ed.) *The Psychology of Computer Vision*, London, McGraw-Hill, pp. 211–7.

5. LUNZER, E. and GARDNER, K. (Eds) (1979) *The Effective Use of Reading*, London, Heinemann Educational Books (for Schools Council).

6. MASON, G.E. and BLANCHARD, J.S. (1979) *Computer Applications in Reading*, Newark, DE, International Reading Association.

7. BALAJTHY, E. (1984) 'Reinforcement and drill by microcomputer', *Reading Teacher*, 37, 5, February, pp. 490–4.

8. NEWMAN, J.M. (1984) 'Language learning and computers', *Language Arts*, 61, 5, September, pp. 494–7.

9. MULLAN, A. (1981) 'Infant words and a sense of adventure', *Educational Computing*, 2, 11, December, pp. 49–51.

10. DUDLEY-MARLING, C.C. (1985) 'Microcomputers, reading and writing: Alternatives to drill and practice', *Reading Teacher*, 38, January, pp. 388–91.

11. CARVER, R.P. and HOFFMAN, J.V. (1981) 'The effect of practice through repeated reading on gain in reading ability using a computer-based instructional system', *Reading Research Quarterly*, 16, 3, pp. 374–90.

12. MEYER, R.S. and CALDWELL, P.A. (1983) 'Transformation', *Computer Education*, [Oxford] 7, 2, pp. 69–78.

13. BURNETT, J.D. and MILLER, L. (1984) 'Computer assisted learning and reading: developing the product or fostering the process', *Computer Education*, [Oxford] 8, 1, pp. 145–50.

14. NEWMAN, J.M. (1984) *op. cit.*

15. LAVENDER, R. (1983) Children using information books', *Education 3–13*, 11, 1, spring pp. 8–12.

16. MOY, B. and RALEIGH, M. (1983) 'Reading for information', *English Magazine*, 11, summer, pp. 27–35.

17. LACY, D. (1983) *op. cit.*

18. LUNZER, E. and GARDNER, K. (Eds). (1979) *op. cit.*, p. 313.

19. MOORE, P.J. (1984) 'Children's metacognitive knowledge about reading: a selected review', *Educational Research*, 24, 2, February, pp. 120–8.

20. LUNZER, E. and GARDNER, K (Eds) (1979) *op. cit.*, pp. 28–9

21. LACY, D. (1983) *op. cit.*

22. See, for instance SMITH, F. (1971) *Understanding Reading: A Psycholinguistic Analysis of Reading and Learning to Read*, London, Holt, Rinehart and Winston.

23. RUDDUCK, J. (1984) *The Sixth Form and Libraries: Problems of Access to Knowledge*, London, British Library.

24. PELLICANO, R.R. (1983) 'Literacy for modern times', *Educational Leadership*, 41, 4, December, pp. 67–9.

25. SMITH, I. (1985) 'Starting off on the write foot', *Guardian*, 2 April, p. 11.

26. CHAMBERS, A. (1973) *Introducing Books to Children*, London, Heinemann Educational Books, p. 22.

27. *Ibid*, p. 23

28. BRITTON, J. (1972) *Language and Learning*, London, Penguin, p. 213.

29. HOGGART, R. (1973) 'Why I value literature', in *About Literature*, volume 2 of *Speaking to Each Other*, London, Penguin, p. 11.

30. TURKLE, S. (1984) *The Second Self: Computers and the Human spirit*. New York, Simon & Schuster, p. 92.
31. CHAMBERS, A. (1973) *op. cit.*, p. 29.
32. RUTHVEN, K. (1984) 'Computer literacy and the curriculum', *British Journal of Educational Studies*, XXXII, 2, June, pp. 134–47.
33. SUHOR, C. (1983) 'Cars, computers and curriculum', *Educational Leadership*, 41, 1, September, pp. 30–2.
34. 'Elements of Computer Literacy' (1984) *Journal of Reading*, 28, 1, October, p. 12.
35. RUTHVEN, K. (1984) *op. cit.*
36. *Ibid*
37. ATHERTON, R. (1980) 'A serious deficiency in school software', *Education Today*, 30, 3, autumn/winter, pp. 14–17; ATHERTON, R. (1982) 'BASIC damages the brain', *Computer Education*, 40, February, pp. 14–17.
38. A clear exposition is found in GOODYEAR, P. (1984) *LOGO: A Guide to Learning Through Programming*, London, Heinemann Computers in Education.
39. EDGAR, J. (1981) 'Language difficulties?', *Times Educational Supplement*, 8 April, p. 44.
40. Helpful chapters on PROLOG can be found in RAMSDEN, E. (Ed.) (1984) *Microcomputers in Education*, Ellis Horwood/Wiley. See especially chapter 5, 'The French connection', by ENNALS R., BOUCELMA, O. and BERGMAN M., pp. 39–49; chapter 6; PROLOG and English teaching', by LATHAM J., pp. 50–5; and chapter 7, 'Computing for everyman or computer applications of micro-PROLOG' by NICHOL, J. with DEAN, J. TOMPSETT, C. and BRIGGS, J. pp. 56–66.
41. SARDELLO, R.J. (1984) 'The technological threat to education', *Teachers College Record*, 85, 4, summer pp 631–9.
42. WAGSCHAL, P.H. (1984) 'A last chance for computers in school?', *Phi Delta Kappan*, 66, 4, December, pp. 251–4.
43. RUTH, D.D. (1981) 'Expanded English: Media study as a basic skill', *NASSP Bulletin*, 65, 444, April, pp. 31–6.
44. FERGUSON, B. (1981) 'Practical work and pedagogy', *Screen Education*, 38, spring, pp. 41–55.
45. KOOL, R. (1980) 'Isolate, inspect, insert', *The B.C. Teacher*, 59, 5, May–June, pp. 184–6.
46. CASSIDY, M. and KNOWLTON, J.Q. (1983) 'Visual literacy: A failed metaphor?', *Educational Communication and Technology Journal*, 31, 2, summer, pp. 67–90.
47. BESWICK, N.W. (1981) 'Visual literacy: A vital skill', *Education Libraries Bulletin*, 24, 1, spring, pp. 29–37.
48. BESWICK, N.W. (1972) *School Resource Centres: The Report of the First Year of the Schools Council Resource Centre Project*, London, Evans/Methuen Educational (Schools Council Working Paper 43). p. 10.

Chapter 5

'The School as Library': Computers in a Context

In chapter 1, many futurological prophecies of what new information technology would do for education were sceptically examined. I suggested that to say something might happen was not at all the same thing as proving it would happen, and that many unexpected developments could, and probably would, divert the path of future history in all manner of unforeseeable ways. I suggested that not every possibility was actually helpful, either to teachers or their students; and that many propositions were based on attitudes to teaching and learning which took no account of factors closest to current educational concern. One instance of this was the emphasis many speculators placed on the 'computer as substitute teacher', a vision of a future education system apparently dependent upon students working through endless networks of 'instructional units', computer-assisted learning packages based on the programmed learning model, ignoring all the widespread and varied testimony to the importance of 'active learning', the steady development of self-confident autonomy, of 'learning to learn', of 'exploration' as a teaching method.

Most teachers are practical people who concentrate on immediately realizable objectives. They do not allow speculation to affect what they actually do in school, however much they may like to fantasize afterwards about what might one day happen. The effects of recent years in British education and society have almost certainly hardened this practical emphasis, especially as 'what might be' sadly always appears to depend on an affluent economy and generous funding for education, two elements which have disappeared almost entirely from view or prospect.

Partly as a result, many teachers are tending, at least in public, to think tactically as much as pedagogically whenever new developments are being considered. This is particularly so in the case of technology and computers, where the overtones of staff-cutting and teacher un-employment are audible in discussions. Moreover, precisely because education authorities have been cutting corners and forcing economies for so long, the very idea of using a machine as a teaching tool brings vivid memories of breakdown, incompetence and humiliation. Our machines have not been properly maintained, we have had to purchase the cheapest models (with inevitable results), technicians to set them up and maintain them have long disappeared, and in-service courses in how to use them have been hard to find and get into.

Yet throughout chapters 2–4 we have seen uses for the new information technology, and have related it to concerns right across the 'active-passive' spectrum of teaching/learning approaches. We have also found implications, in a changing society and in the world of changing knowledge, for using a wide range of such approaches and particularly for using technology to release the learner from 'inauthentic labour' and from the constraints of 'instruction'.

Even with the technology we have at present, schools and classrooms could be very different. (Assume that the pace of change continues, and the prospects are staggering: so staggering that, as we saw in chapter 1, it is idle to consider them too seriously — there are too many unknowns.) It is a sad fact that education always has to lag behind, waiting its turn and at the mercy of the most aggressive marketing forces; and in recent years we have lagged further than we ever expected. But suppose, just for a few pages, that we did not: assume, briefly, that suddenly the education profession was given unlimited funds and told to get cracking. What might the result look like, bearing in mind what we have seen so far?

(If such exercises make you nervous or suspicious, worry not. Reality and critical scepticism will return, devastatingly, before the chapter ends. But remember one thing: I shall not be inventing any new technology: everything hereunder could, in theory, be done today, given the will, the money, the people and the accompanying software.)

1 Would we have schools at all?

Maybe education could happen at home? Perhaps all children could be issued with their own keyboards, visual display units and printers, video recorders and whatever else; and perhaps we could educate them by some new amalgamation of 'distance teaching' (Open University style), 'teacher-broadcasters' as in the Australian outback (for continuity and 'personal bonding'), and perhaps also children communicating with one another by electronic mail or by Citizens Band radio.

Unless homes and families had by some equally miraculous decree become uniformly perfect, we would call this idea a non-starter — though we might bear in mind some aspect of high-tech home education, as and when helpful. However, new technology makes it easier to come to acceptable arrangements with those parents who at present withdraw their children and insist on teaching them at home (Roland Meighan has written extensively on this group). For the rest, the great majority, the social aspects of education would continue to be best developed in school-like settings; and quite a lot of the active information-seeking we would want to encourage and train would be best learnt in purpose-built accommodation.

2   So what would schools be like?

Surely, very much more flexible than now, and heavily resourced: a wide range of hardware and software chosen for simplicity and sturdiness as well as for its educational potential. In each classroom, every pupil could have an individual 'work-station' (we used to call them 'desks'), with computer terminal, and screen, adapted to receive video or film as well as computer programs; moving and still pictures could be accessed from videodisc or conventional film or tape. Commentary or music would be listened to on headphones without disturbing anyone else. The teacher too, of course, would have similar equipment, including controls to monitor or intervene anywhere in the class. We know how to do all this, given the money and will.

Children could be linked in many ways. First, all workstations in one 'class' would be linked to the teacher's control unit. But then pupils could be variously linked together, so that group activities could be undertaken, of whatever size might seem desirable (from two upwards) at any particular time, and people could join or leave as needed. The teacher could present units of material to an entire class, using the VDU's as a combined blackboard and AV screen; or to only a selection, concentrating on some individuals, while others were working separately or in groups on their own projects. When not in use, the VDU screens and terminals would fold away to allow for other activities to take place instead — including many of the traditional elements of today's schooling. And unlike language laboratories, all this would not be limited to one subject or one type of activity.

3   Adjacent areas.

According to the level of schooling, we could provide specialist areas, for instance for lab work, craft design technology, needlework and fashion, and domestic arts. There would be proper gymnasia with genuine challenges to young bodies; rooms for drama, including video facilities so that drama work could be related to, or integrated with, practical work in media studies; music rooms with both traditional and modern instrumentation (and soundproofing); and a separate library resource area or areas, where individual or small group work could continue exploring the full range of information media currently available.

4   The library resource area.

This would be very different from even the most elaborate current model for one significant reason: the school would itself be so saturated with information resources that in a very real sense you could say, not 'we have a library resource area in our school' but 'our school is itself a library resource organization'. From each individual work-station in the 'home-base' classroom (you will notice that my model is not so revolutionary as to abolish that) it would be possible to access a colossal range of information and study materials. The teacher could call up videos, programs, individual still pictures, recorded sound or whatever, and, when appropriate, so could the pupil. The technology to do this already exists; I saw a very primitive version in operation in a large senior high school in Chicago in 1966, for audiotapes, and students could access them over their own home telephones as well as in school!

Some of the material called up would exist physically within the school, perhaps in a central resource collection; much else could be accessed over a telephone line from local, regional, national or even international collections, assuming somebody had the will to apply the technology in practice. A 'library resource area' would be equally served, but would also contain items unique to it: I suspect that these items would be special and individual in usage — large maps and charts to pore over, music recordings to listen to at length, and books for prolonged and intensive reading. Maybe we should include films or videos, studied alone. And at present, until the task of transferring them all to computerized form has been accomplished (if it ever is) the library would contain the major encyclopaedias, dictionaries, abstracts, indexes and catalogues, many of which schools cannot at present afford. Also available (but see the next paragraph) would be specialist expertise in the process of search, enquiry, 'information retrieval' and project strategy.

5 Staff.

And who, you are asking, is going to look after all this and make sure it works? We would need a full complement of teachers (let who can provide the formula — research is very ambivalent) and undoubtedly we would need appropriate ancillary staffing. Computer terminals have very few moving parts and there is nothing like the propensity for breakdown that is found at present with (say) projectors and tape recorders (or language laboratories), but certainly some technician help would be necessary. (Shortly after writing these words my own BBC B keyboard refused to function, needing quick replacement of a small connection!) The best existing model of ancillary support here is that of the Inner London Education Authority 'media resource officer', able to do first-line maintenance but also well skilled at other, more creative tasks such as resource design and production. The long-standing argument about what sort of person runs the library resource area would continue, but two requirements are obvious: a thorough understanding of information technology and the organization of knowledge, and a job description placing such expertise full-time in library resources. Given those two requirements, it would clearly be advantageous for the person con-cerned to have as much education background as possible.

It is my guess, which the reader might like to think into and check, that the availability of so much resource material 'on line' (whether it be computer programs or verbal data or audio-visual items) would make the ancillary staffing load much less than in previous periods might have been expected, given the breadth and depth of information provision.

> ... Let us pause and look at what we have so far.

Any speculation of this kind is necessarily partial and individual. Almost any teacher reading the above paragraphs will be fidgeting and muttering 'What about X?' and 'Predictably he's underestimated Y'. Of course: only a planning committee could include everything and get the balance right, and I am far from suggesting that we have reached the stage for one of those.

What matters is that every item mentioned is technologically possible now, with equipment currently on sale (at a price). Software would have to be written; money, machines and personnel would have to be found (and many people retrained). But in terms of technological possibility, my 'school as library' vision is not fantasy and it is not futurology, except sociologically; indeed, there are almost certainly some technological developments I have overlooked, underemphasized or misunderstood.

What tomorrow's world makes further possible we must wait and see, but in the meantime, supposing the current vision were actually realizable in some sufficiently well-resourced form, what would this mean? There would certainly be management implications, calls for the design of organizational structures (within schools, between schools, within LEAs, nationally, and so on), and we will examine these in later pages and in the last chapter. But at this point we might like to ask ourselves three questions:

— If we had such a highly resourced model of an education system realized for us, would we know what to do with it?
— Does it represent a possible future we might actually want?
— Assuming appropriate funding for in-service training and support staff, could we actually refuse it as a gift?

I repeat: the technology is here now. What would happen if the money to support its use was available as well?

I suggest we start by looking as positively as we dare, letting in a few caveats on the way: before coming back to the very different world of current reality and seeing whether we have learnt anything in the process.

The Well-Resourced Teacher

The advantages for the teacher of our 'information-rich' school, the 'school as library', can be listed fairly easily:

1   Teachers would have ready access to high-quality material for their own 'presentation' sessions, i.e. those occasions when they judged it best to put across a unit of the syllabus in direct class teaching.

Not only would they be able to access (say) films or videos: even the maps, diagrams, charts, graphs or photographs they needed could be (at least in theory) called up on screen. Those sessions with the spirit duplicator would disappear when the same item could either be summoned to appear on each vou in the class or else be printed out in multiple copies on the printer. Moreover, teachers could amend and improve them to fit personal need, before releasing them to the class — all by use of terminal and monitor.

2   Teachers would also be able to plan a wider range of activity sessions, because of the quantity of support material they could access for the class to use, either individually or in groups.

Some of this material would be similar to items in 1 above, but used for purposes planned by teachers with their own class in mind ('Using this map ...' or 'Using these population statistics ...' or 'Look carefully at this picture and ...'). Other material might be the 'information media' equivalent of the good resource pack: well-produced examples of learning activities planned by expert teachers elsewhere, perhaps as part of a curriculum project.

3   Teachers could plan activities that made direct use of the terminals themselves as teaching tools: the class working on their keyboards to practise the skills or generate the data — as in a LOGO exercise or statistical computation, or the use in word-processing mode of the keyboard-as-writing-tool.

We saw earlier that more and more activities lend themselves at some stage to the kinds of activity which a computer terminal makes possible. Some of it might, very properly, be drill and reinforcement — in a wide context of other activities at other times.

4   Teachers could also plan activities which directly taught and practised enquiry and research skills, knowing that in the individual terminal at each 'work-station' was a major tool for information-seeking, together with access to a phenomenal range of data.

The previous snag with 'projects', that because of depleted resources in classroom, school library and public library branch, what resulted was often as much the result of chance and good or bad luck, would disappear once each desk was 'on line' to wider sources elsewhere easily brought to personal access on the desk screen.

5   Some of the current sources of behaviour problems in schools would be eliminated or side-stepped.

Potential trouble-moments arise when teachers turn away to collect and distribute textbooks from the cupboard, or load projectors or erect screens, or when unruly children roam corridors en route to the library. Such occasions would no longer necessarily arise with direct screen access for both teacher and class.

However, as we saw in earlier chapters, this glossy vision is not entirely without its problems. There is little evidence that teachers as a whole actually want to have ready access to huge quantities of material. Even before computers, it would have been possible to provide coordinated data, readily accessible, about the wide range of print and audiovisual items available by purchase or by loan from local sources. At any one time there are some 40 000 school textbooks in print, from anything up to 2000 publishing sources. Teachers make do by a very random system of collecting such publishers' catalogues as are known to them, and although some local education authorities attempt to provide exhibitions and visits to major book suppliers, teachers' behaviour in book selection is (for whatever reason — perhaps the long tradition of LEA neglect) much more haphazard than might be supposed. (The necessity for the Lady David Report[1] strongly implies this without saying so outright.) For over twenty years the University of London Institute of Education Library has housed the National Textbook Reference Library (now the National Reference Library of Schoolbooks and Classroom Materials) but its use by teachers has not up to now been what was envisaged and hoped for.

Some efforts have been made to improve bibliographic coverage of textbook and other educational materials, but most have failed from lack of interest. The Council for Educational Technology, for instance, produced HELPIS (Higher Education Learning Programmes Information Service), offering teachers in the tertiary sector information about locally-produced resource materials which could be borrowed without fuss; it soon died. Some teachers centres during the 1970s briefly tried to build up information networks of local resources, addresses, useful people to contact. Teachers do not know of 'British National Bibliography', just as most of them do not know of 'British Education Index', and the various journals attempting to cover audiovisual materials have been financially insecure and by no means widely available in schools. Few schools have devised systems within their walls so that such bibliographic and other knowledge available among the staff is pooled, stored and shared; attempts were sometimes made during the 1970s in school resource centres, but this was usually the side of the work that was abandoned first when 'the cuts' began to bite. Teachers have generally preferred to select their materials from a small sample of catalogues and reviewing magazines, giving the distinct impression that anything more elaborate would undermine their professional sense of security.

Thus a sceptic might reasonably guess that what teachers would value about the 'information-rich' model might well be the certainty of access to a few trusted items, rather than the availability of a great quantity. Teachers go very much by personal experience and inspection (and have little time to inspect more than a small proportion), supplemented by word of mouth recommendation. How many schools wanted the *British Catalogue of Audiovisual Materials*, bemoaned its lack before it appeared, or tried to purchase it when the British Library Bibliographic Services Division finally produced it at the start of the present decade? When it was made available for searching on-line, how many teachers knew or were interested — and how many have bemoaned its demise?

The British education system gives a great measure of curricular autonomy to individual schools and to individual teachers in their classrooms — even today, when the dragon of national control looms ever larger. Yet not only do teachers lack access to information about the basic tools of the curriculum (textbooks, resources, audiovisual media, computer programs) in any systematic way, there is no strong evidence that they feel the loss or would welcome the opportunity. Such access would face them with intimidating choices: What do I look for? How do I know what is worth calling up? How do I find the time to assess it first? What might I have to decide about it? Why don't I just 'teach it my way'? Thus resources get produced, with great labour, while high quality examples are actually easily available nearby.

Yet these were doubts that arose in previous 'revolutions'. Teachers slowly adapted to looking out audio-cassettes, checking times of schools broadcasts, setting the timer for the video, and preparing the accompanying handouts. Steadily, if very slowly, the effects of high quality back-up stock have percolated through the system. But it will be the certainty of delivery, not the huge spread of possibility, that will attract support. Will it lead (as some fear) to an inevitable deskilling of the teacher? Only if one thinks that the widespread availability of Durell's maths texts in the 1930s and 1940s had the same effect. For bad teachers, perhaps they did: for others, they clearly represented a general consensus view and freed teachers from the need to make their own texts, leaving them time to do what only the individual professional in the classroom can do — attend to individual need.

The Well-Resourced Learner

There are obvious lessons we can learn from these last comments, but before we draw them let us turn to the situation for the student.

Whereas teachers could probably cope — by inertia — in a heavily resourced situation, for their straight teaching needs, it is when we bring in the activity of the students that the opportunities grow and the problems with them.

1   Because of the range of information available to the teacher, students can expect to be engaged in activities more closely related to individual need and interest. In enquiry projects, the 'failure to find out' could be practically eliminated, and work ranging from the small exercise to the big individual project be entered into with confidence.

A lecturer colleague of mine once found that his son had been set homework to find information which was available only in specific back numbers of the *National Geographic Magazine*, not held in the school library, nor in the local branch public library, but only in the central library reference department two bus routes away and closing at 7:00pm — but that none of this latter information had been first researched by the class teacher. Such pre-checking would be relatively easy under our speculative model.

2   There is necessarily a 'search strategy' element in working with resources accessed on-line from school or other collections. Prestel for instance is normally searched through a step by step method, which forces the enquirer to conceptualize need and work through a hierarchically organized structure. The same is true with other data banks, however differently arranged. The SIR package, limited though it is, teaches the student to articulate the stages of enquiry, as do similar packages.

Here the student, however, comes up against the same problems as the teacher: how do I choose which data banks to search? how do I select from the multiple items I find? I asked in chapter 1 how the inexperienced learner who couldn't cope well with just one book would cope with access to many millions, and this remains the problem. The answer, obviously, is to devize intermediate systems, as we shall see later.

3   The student too would benefit from being able to work from a 'work-station' that gave facilities to work on data and manipulate it, as well as retrieve it in a variety of forms.

This remains the major advantage for the student of the new technology in its fullest form. The great problem with much schoolwork at present, in both the formal and less formal modes, is the quantity of unnecessary or 'inauthentic' labour involved in so many assignments. Once we accept the computer, not as teacher, but as multiple tool, we move into a whole new way of thinking about planning learning. Even though a sufficient number of 'instructional programs to match the needs of all levels of learner' is never going to be available (and we can take this as being a reasonable assumption), it need not trouble us one jot. Pianos ('interactive' devices which allow perceptive users to ask 'what if . . .?') are still valuable despite severe limitations on the variety of sheet music producible to match every mood, every need and every level of skill. What is sad is that so few aspiring pianists are taught how to improvize and explore the instrument and the world of music for themselves.

At this point most practical readers will be restlessly leafing ahead to see when we are returning to the 'real world'. Was not chapter 1 gently ridiculing the futurologists and is not this chapter falling into precisely the same trap? Even if the technology exists already, surely this is pure theory, and therefore pure speculation, if the financial muscle and the professional will are lacking? Of course: but precisely because this model does not depend on technology yet to be invented, we can in fact prepare for the arrival of some bits of that technology in our schools, classrooms and libraries, and begin thinking now about what we would do with it (or for that matter, how we would resist its introduction if that's how we feel). There are schools already, in this country, where identifiable elements of 'the school as library' can be seen.

(Meanwhile let me remind computer buffs that it is the continuing beauty of the codex book format that one actually can leaf ahead, and back, and later return, and find the text still there to use as one wants and not as the programmer prescribes.)

What emerged most strongly from the brief analysis of this chapter so far is that we, or somebody, must address the problem of quantity. Apart from money and time, the worst headache facing the teacher in the 'information-rich' setting of our 'school as library' is the fear of being plunged into an undifferentiated jungle of information resources, many of which may be unsuitable for our needs, poorly constructed, devised on bad pedagogical principles, or leaving too many problems unanswered. For the first time, we have not too little but very much too much — and if a respected American institution labels nearly two-thirds of them 'DO NOT CONSIDER', we feel bound, as good consumerists, to be on our guard.

And if this is so for teachers, who presumably have some guidelines on what to look for, how much worse must it be for students? All very well to speak of students 'making their own meaning' and 'finding their own information', but what do we do if some of it is palpably racist and much else based on an improper or insecure foundation?

Clearly there must be different levels of access. For students, it would be beneficial if what they first searched was not the widest international data base but something much more manageable. First there must be the actual physical resources (books, atlases, videos, programs, models) which can be seen, handled and used on the spot in school. An index of these items (on screen if that is the prevailing mode) then enables the student to make the connection, grasp the relationship, between physical resources and their index description. When occasion suggests that items not now in school be sought and accessed, they can undertake the next step, which is searching an appropriate data base devized with the needs of education in mind. Perhaps this is where local education authorities should devize their own second-stage data banks, perhaps based on the catalogues of Schools Library Service collections. I also think of the printed lists of recommended books which school districts in the USA often produce for the use of schools in areas where libraries and bookshops alike are non-existent. Such lists on-line would be cheaper to access and quicker to up-date.

We don't at present have these 'intermediate level' data banks, nor do we have (you will be insisting) on-line access to the LEA film library; but now that the technology itself exists, in theory, some-body should be working on practical adaptations that would bring the possibility nearer reality. (The Chicago audio-tape scheme I men-tioned on page 95 selected the dialled tape by number, made a quick copy in 30 seconds, and then transmitted the copy, so that the original was still available. Multiply the number of phone lines by the number of required copiers, to begin with, and some idea of the problem may be grasped. Is it sufficiently valuable? I suggest we might see how near we can sensibly get, because of the very great convenience.) One of the most practical services to schools, teachers and students might be the development of different levels of data-bank provision and electronic delivery systems: something between the resource centre's catalogue and BLAISE, the British Library's multi-million automated on-line catalogue, and between the present labour intensive postal service and instant electronic delivery, to enable sensible enquiry to be planned and to proceed.

Perhaps the needs of teachers should be tackled first (on the principle that to help them is also to help students) and this might include a data base with information teachers often ask for — age level of intended audience, ability-range if known, vocabulary level, and some guide to other people's evaluation. It is up to other services to decide how much data it is sensible to offer, how many items teachers would tolerate being faced with at one time, and to be the acceptable interface between schools and the infinite availability outside.

The Future is Now But ...

So far we have tried to analyze our 'information-rich' 'school as library' model optimistically. At first it sounds marvellous to think of only having to press a few keys and dial a few numbers to get anything one needs — especially to the teacher or student labouring in institutions that are, in sharp contrast, 'information-poor'. We suggested that a first step would be to tackle what is in any case a practical problem, the sheer quantity of material currently available, and plan some kind of filtering system that would make access to what one is really likely to need less formidable.

But how about the rest of the model? We saw that there were modest advantages to the teacher, but that teachers did not appear actually to be clamouring for such advantages. Meanwhile, 'a workstation for every pupil'? Is it right that we should divert money from other pressing demands to the purchase of equipment which might, within a very few years, become obsolescent, and about whose use there is still (as we saw) controversy? As I write these words, one could purchase, for the cost of one BBC B micro, well over 100 books, instantly usable and reusable, which even if they only do one thing, do that thing extremely well and have stood the test of time. For 'books' read, for that matter, any similar item which in these hard-pressed times is in desperately short supply. Add to that the cost (which did not appear in earlier pages of this chapter) of multiple telephone lines — however many would we need? Even one per classroom is far more than schools currently have (though it is taken for granted that lecturers in colleges and universities will have internal and external phones in their own offices) and if we add a fair number extra to allow for (supervised?) student access to outside data sources, the number shoots up.

Now, it may well be that eventually we shall find ourselves in a future which has precisely this kind of multiple provision. Arthur C. Clarke somewhere quotes an American spokesman, at the time of the invention of the telephone, who saw a marvellous future for this new instrument; eventually it was quite likely that 'every big city would have one'. Another pundit once saw no future for motor cars outside cities — it was obvious, the American rural areas didn't have roads for the cars to drive on! So perhaps our ideas of what is possible are just as over-cautious. However, we have been deliberately eschewing prophecy in these pages; we are concerned with decision, on the basis of present possibility.

There are some assertions we can at least tentatively make:

1   There is no case at present for totally abandoning other items of expenditure simply in order to fill our schools with computer hardware and software.

The 'all-embracing software' is not in sight, and offers no educational advantage.

2   Computer purchasing must therefore take place in the total context of school resourcing, and must compete for available funds with other demands.

This is likely to mean that development will be rather slow, and that the traditional schools will quickly reach what they see as a plateau beyond which further provision is unnecessary (enough perhaps to enable computer studies classes to do practical work in one special room). It also means that computer purchasing will compete not only with books and chalk and paper, but also with projectors and video and kilns and pottery wheels and metalwork tools, with some of which it will compare favourably enough in purely financial terms. Wealthy areas get the parents' association to chip in with donations for fashionable items. However, in the poorer authorities such bonuses do not arrive, and the funds are admittedly tiny enough to cause genuine concern.

3   Schools may be considering computer purchasing under two major headings:
    (a)   use in classroom teaching, ie within the context of a class lesson under the direct supervision of a teacher;
    (b)   use 'across the school', for organization (for example, listing, planning, cataloguing, timetabling) and for general access, especially to pupils in informal circumstances, such as in the library at breaks or lunch time.

These two categories are not wholly separable, inasmuch as with careful planning machines can be moved around and shared, but may be conceptually useful in making clear the different functions information technology can serve. In some cases equipment will have to be dedicated to one function in one place.

4   Information technology should not be thought of only in terms of use of stand-alone machines but also considered in terms of systems. Facilities such as Econet and Prestel greatly expand the usefulness of what one already has. The costs of linking micros together, of electronic mail facilities, and modem access to other sources, are not so great as to preclude their prudent use within reasonable constraints.

This can be achieved without jumping immediately into costly and unproven commitments, of the kind outlined in our 'model'. At the same time, each example moves a step further towards the achievement of that model, if and when the school is ready to attempt it. Obviously it will be more difficult in less affluent authorities.

5   Although 'instructional' uses of the micro-computer are still prominent, both in the available software and in the literature of the subject, such uses only duplicate what teachers are already doing. The most useful direction for a school to take with its use of computer technology is learner-centred activities.

I quoted Abbott's 'continuum', from Instructional through Revelatory and Conjectural to Emancipatory (discussed in Kent[2]), reminding us of the 'passive-active' continuum in chapter 2. It is this 'emancipatory' facility of new information technology which seems, on the balance of arguments rehearsed so far, to be the most impressive and the most persuasive. As the pressures build to shift emphasis from instruction to enquiry, from teaching of subject content alone to concurrent mastery of learning skills, the unique attributes of IT make use within the school's learning programme increasingly important.

In sum, therefore, we look for a phased introduction of computers into our schools, not to be trendy and certainly not in order to economize on staff or on staff time, but because we are impelled to move, for good pedagogic as well as social reasons, towards those styles of learning which such information tools can most helpfully stimulate and facilitate. This means that we are unlikely to be able to say, in a year or two, 'We have enough', because the more adventurous, learner-centred activities will always soak up more and more of them (until something else comes along to do the work even better). It is not a matter of fitting out one classroom, although that may be one interim measure in some schools.

The more such provision we have, and the more we are able to adopt such pedagogic styles, the nearer we come in fact to the picture drawn at the start of this chapter, though not necessarily in that glamorous and dramatic form. Yet the 'school as library' is not, when examined closely, a matter of quantity of provision; it is brought about by organization; it is system. Imagine, for a moment, the wealth of provision suggested a few pages back, but without any overall coordination or planning; imagine teachers, or departments, working with such wealth of materials but without reference to the rest of the school, and imagine outside agencies setting up on-line and other provision without consultation or regard to other decision-making. Now imagine what can be achieved — what is, in some schools, being achieved — in the maximization of use of whatever it is one has, by careful and sensitive coordinative action. We can have 'the school as library' and with it, proceed cautiously and expeditiously towards the 'information-rich' education system.

A Structure for Achievement

Many teachers mistrust the idea of coordinated systems and prefer to rely on their own trusted private cupboard of resources and gadgets. Yet 'coordination' is not a synonym for 'centralization'. It implies only that a school decides to treat its equipment and resources as one collection, no matter where housed, and to try to make it easier for those who may need any of it to have some kind of access, with any necessary safeguards. What is initially required is that useful data be gathered of what is available where, and the circumstances of its present use. This data can form the basis of agreed decisions about what should ensue: what should stay put, what (if anything) could without too much sacrifice be relocated, and where, and what considerations should go into a sensible sharing system. The usual pattern, where such organization has proved reasonably successful, has included major pooled collections for common use together with smaller collections in special areas (departments, wings, separate buildings) as necessary, and smaller personal collections in the day-to-day control of individuals.

The fact that some proposed models of resource coordination have come from groups representing a library interest[3] has led to sinister hints of a 'library takeover'. There seems no reason to suppose that such a takeover would be anything but benign, but in fact no 'takeover' is required. While libraries exist in schools they can hardly be left out of any coordinating system (they are usually the largest single contributors) and have the advantage that their motivation is as altruistic as could be expected: they exist to serve other people, not themselves, and in that sense are a useful counter to departmental lobbying and sectional in-fighting. The widespread appointments (in the shire counties) of senior teaching staff to Head of Resources posts, makes the necessary and important link between the coordination of facilities and the coordination of curriculum. What can properly be emphasized, however, is that the expertise for the development of systems underpinning resource coordination is most typically and easily found among professionals in library and information work. (A caveat: if you are able to appoint such people, look for the same personal qualities as you would seek in a lively teacher — enthusiasm, ability to communicate, out-goingness, responsibility.)

The good news is that what was once the sheer labour of developing information systems within resource organizations (see my case studies,[4]) can now be greatly reduced with the aid of the computer as an administrative tool. Once, we had the choice of multi-page typed lists which were quickly outdated by new additions, or card catalogues in filing drawers which could only be centrally located and therefore had to be deliberately visited. A computer catalogue can be updated very speedily (it does its own filing), can generate lists through a printer at the touch of a key (and the lists can be total or partial according to need), can in theory be accessed from many different terminals with appropriate linking, and can be programmed so that the enquirer can search by author, title, keyword, name of machine, date of production, level of audience or whatever. The multiple access sought in the 1970s by those long-forgotten users of optical coincidence punched cards is now here in electronic form, and will be welcomed.

The bad news is that the smaller microcomputers are not suited to the more elaborate functions set out in the previous paragraph, and that appropriate programs still need to be written. There are 'school library catalogue' programs, notably for the primary sector, but they are very simple and have severe memory limitations. Tomorrow may be different. (I may add that I have inspected some computer catalogues in libraries of large academic institutions I had better not name, and found them largely dedicated to the convenience of the cataloguing department rather than the service of users. No doubt this is prompted by economic constraints, but I find it deplorable nonetheless. We need to establish our objectives very clearly and insist upon them.) It will probably be better, in the short run, to use the smaller micros for equipment listings, departmental catalogues and specific-subject bibliographies. If prices continue to come down in real terms, it may soon be possible to gain access to more powerful business machines (to name names is unnecessary) which with a hard disc would meet the likely needs of most medium-size schools; programs such as MIRABILIS (from the University of London Central Information Service) suitably modified, would be worth investigating in that case, with a 20 000 record capacity and well-planned facility to search on many different 'fields'. But that is for the (possible) future.

To know what you have is the first essential; the second is to work out a sensitive system of sharing that does not too greatly threaten the teacher's sense of professional autonomy, and in secondary schools that of his department. This is where many promising schemes broke down over the last decade, particularly if staff changes meant they were no longer backed and/or underpinned by a senior and powerful person. Where curriculum changes were being forced through in the teeth of staff opposition, the resource organization was often the point on which this opposition focussed most effectively. In one well-known example, the head's insistence that a specified proportion of each department's fund be spent 'in the library resources area' aroused particular fury, and when a new head took over not only this proposal but the entire thrust for curriculum innovation was quietly dropped.

The purpose of coordination, sharing, planning, is to maximise the effectiveness of whatever books, resources, equipment and expertise is available. Schools which have a long-standing tradition of this kind have come more successfully through the long years of economic stringency than those who have preferred to maintain traditional patterns, particularly the departmentalized pattern of the secondary sector. What brings the advantages is not just the system of coordination itself, but the habit induced of planning in whole-school rather than departmental terms. In times of constraint it is rarely possible for one department or one group of teachers to succeed both in innovating and at the same time bringing large-scale financial benefit; yet by whole-school planning (with consent) developments can be planned, often in stages, which change the whole stance of the school at a relatively modest cost.

Earlier chapters highlighted the importance of whole-school policies for the development of learning skills and the various literacies. Many contemporary pressures can be best dealt with in this fashion. If a school is to meet the aspirations of the movements for language across the curriculum, anti-racist and multicultural policies, and the development of well-planned enquiry methodologies, it must act together as a school, not leave things to the varying whims of departments, each of whom has its own and different list of priorities. Such planning is difficult to achieve by agreement, and is very vulnerable to staff conference filibusters, but many would now agree on its importance as schools face the challenges of change alongside the equal challenges of staff losses and diminished funding. One small practical example of what may emerge from such whole-school planning is an agreement to subscribe to Prestel, and to place it in the library resource area, for curricular and cross-departmental reasons: when perhaps the subscription would otherwise have taken an undue slice out of the library allocation as such.

Whole-school policy-making this kind, requiring participation and the winning of consent, makes heavy demands on the headteacher and senior staff, who will feel they need every scrap of encouragement from local advisers, the LEA, and HMI.

Much of the work that initially resulted from the 'Bruner impetus', attempting to plan curricula to stimulate guided discovery, took place in backgrounds less unified and coordinated than this. I suggest that planning for methodological variety requires such whole-school co-operation: that in planning such curricula, the 'school as library' becomes a key element in success: that new technology offers improved chances of success, in collaboration with the old: and that this may help to temper the scepticism with which such aspirations have previously been greeted.

The Insufficiency of Structures

All this can be made to sound very well, and there are some writers on education whose major response to criticism is to re-jig their presentations, rather as some advertisers and politicians fiddle with emphases and images, instead of rethinking the content. There is a long and respectable history of experimentation with different methods of planning and management within schools, and for fifteen years and more I have advised, counselled, and consulted on the resource organization aspect, here and overseas. Certainly the economic climate has changed during that time, and there have been changes in dominant aims and objectives; rereading the policy documents with which, over the years, I have been involved or to which I have turned for support and guidance reveal such changes, and I hope also show that those involved were learning from experience. Yet the final testimony is clear enough: that establishing administrative structures as such does not automatically produce the answers or solve the major questions (though it may resolve some of them).

This indeed is why from time to time this book has emphasized whole-school planning and discussion, has drawn attention to drawbacks and contrary indications, and included cautious or uneasy phrases and sentences. This 'school as library' chapter has been written with the vivid memory of visits to local authorities, school districts and schools themselves where on the surface it would seem they had everything right, organized with first class support — and yet what was happening showed all too clearly the age-old finding, 'no significant difference'. Equally there have been places where, by dint of extraordinary efforts by extraordinary people with extraordinary dedication and skill, exciting results were obtained without either the resources to organize or the apparent need for consultation. What does one say in the face of such contrasts?

First, one cannot legislate on a basis of extraordinary people, nor indeed can one necessarily look at their past history and find infallible ways of producing them. Most teachers are talented, and reasonably dedicated, but are neither geniuses nor compulsive workaholics; recent years have shown that there are limits to their patience. So planning must assume an averagely talented, averagely motivated workforce — and remember that part of the 'pace of change' everyone talks about is a plethora of reports and royal commissions and policy documents which demand of this workforce an unusual resilience and flexibility. Few people can tolerate for long periods the alertness, creativity and excitement which novelty generates on its first appearance, and teachers are faced with doing a job which makes constant personal and professional demands even without that novelty. To have to live, year in year out, on the very frontiers of professional rethinking is exhausting and likely to lead, inevitably, to resistance.

From this one can sensibly conclude that anything calculated to ease the 'anxiety of change' would be welcomed by teachers, and in theory a 'whole-school policy' for resources deployment and curriculum planning aims to give that help and security. In practice there are several factors that bring about the reverse. Present financial constraints, for instance, mean that even with the most careful planning and consultation, some types of provision cannot be made. Some of them will be emotionally significant to particular teachers (for perfectly honourable reasons) and the system gets a negative mark. Moreover, in such circumstances administrative snags multiply: a film borrowed as a substitute for whatever was turned down fails to arrive on time; equipment not replaced breaks down at a crucial moment; a project loan ordered by a teacher reluctant enough to attempt project work in any case turns out to be insufficient or aimed at the wrong age-group or not available till next term.

Even when supply is not the problem, the teacher may well feel insecure. The equipment may be sufficiently unfamiliar to cause anxiety — and that anxiety is immediately perceived by a difficult class. The new methodology (whatever it is) may have been insufficiently thought through, and the teacher feel totally at a loss when some of the class respond in totally unexpected ways. The team pre-planning may have overlooked assumptions one teacher thought too obvious to mention, with the result that essential content is missed or one unit takes three times as long to complete. Outside events, over which the school has no control whatever, can complicate a programme or wipe it out altogether: total loss of electric power (from natural or human causes), epidemics, unexpected holidays on successive Mondays, or whatever. On their own, each of these hazards is relatively trivial and its problems easily resolved; added to the pressures of constant novelty, and cumulating through the school year, they set up resistance and resentment, for which the easiest target is the administration or that element which most readily symbolizes their frustration.

Resource-using methods, even resource-based teaching with relatively simple equipment such as the overhead projector, are more complicated than the old lecture/questions/exercises sequence; the further one goes along the 'passive-active continuum', the more variables are being introduced and the more triggers for concern. Thus it is commonplace to find (and in earlier chapters I gave examples from the literature) that teachers set to initiate new and (to them) innovative programmes after a careful and lengthy briefing will tend to begin in the most cautious way circumstances allow: the Queensland geography teachers still anxious to 'cover the subject matter content', or the Midlands users of the General Studies Project material who used 'resources for learning' only as 'teaching aids'. It is hard to blame them: the point is to take their natural professional conservatism into account in the whole-school planning.

Few teachers entered the profession because they 'felt they had a talent for managing groups in the enquiry mode using computers in association with other information sources'. Most came because they could envisage themselves 'controlling and instructing a class'. The more teachers feel under pressure, the more they will 'revert to type' and to the traditional methods which, within very clear limitations, 'succeed', at least for some of the pupils and for some learning objectives.

To say all this isn't negative: on the contrary, it helps to point to what will be necessary for positive success. Provision of materials, equipment, marvellous communication devices and technical help will not, in itself, do more than complicate our schools; detailed 'whole-school' planning and policies, valuable though they are, will not in themselves win more than temporary consent. If we think we know what are the directions in which all these factors should be leading us, we have next to consider the detail of what else is required. This is the subject matter of our final chapter.

NOTES

1. *The Supply of Books to Schools and Colleges*, report of the Committee of Enquiry under the chairmanship of Baroness David, Booksellers Association/Publishers Association, 1981. See also. VINCENT, K. (1980) *A Survey of Methods by Which Teachers Select Books*, Sheffield, University of Sheffield, Centre for Research on User Studies.
2. KENT, A. (1985) The challenge of the microcomputer. in: GRAVES, N.J. (Ed.) *Geography in Education Now*, 2nd edn, London, University of London Institute of Education (Bedford Way Paper 13), pp. 32–50.
3. Library Association. (1977) *Library Resource Provision in Schools: Guidelines and Recommendations*, London, Library Association; School Library Association. (1980) *The Way Ahead: The Organisation and Staffing of Libraries and Learning Resources in Schools in the 1980s*, London, School Library Association.
4. BESWICK, N.W. (1975) *Organising Resources: Six Case Studies*, final report of the Schools Council Resource Centre Project, London, Heinemann Educational Books.

Chapter 6

Next Steps, For Teachers and Those Who Help Them

New information technology gives a marvellous opportunity for all of us to rethink the education system and its priorities, and to re-examine some long-cherished hopes and objectives. What it does not do is provide imperative answers. We are still left with choices that have to be made on the basis of insufficient evidence, just as we always were. Previous chapters concluded that there were good grounds for choosing to re-examine enquiry as a mode — enquiry-based teaching leading on to enquiry-based learning, with students in quest — on the basis of the improved possibilities offered by a combination of old and new information technologies. Moreover, I suggested that the framework should be the acquisition of the skills necessary to retrieve information and construct meaning by the use of the new technology, and that this might help to remove one of the principal complaints against the enquiry method in the past — that it lacked focus, that the evidential basis for its supposed advantages was insecure, and that it was hard for the teacher to know what if anything was succeeding. As most so-called 'information skills' are conceptual rather than mechanical, their development across many curriculum subjects gives structure to an otherwise apparently amorphous method. Computers and information can be integrated within curriculum to make active 'the use of knowing'.

It is not enough, however, simply to commend enquiry methods to those readers who are class teachers, append some readings and hope for the best. Teachers will point out, acidly, that many worthwhile schemes in education are simply not happening because they lack the staff power, the materials and equipment, the ancillary help, the advisory support, the in-service know-how, the back-up facilities and, above all, the time to get things going and maintain a reasonable level of control over the result. Once upon a time it was possible to visit schools as a consultant and show ways in which, by a re-adjustment of what was already present and available, significant improvements in possibility could be brought about. This is no longer the case; recent years have seen drastic worsening of provision in almost all sectors, and it is not acceptable any longer for governments to fall back on the defence that 'falling rolls' necessarily mean cuts in provision. There is a basic minimum provision which all schools must have: if staff is cut, do we cut the English teacher or the maths teacher? If we must now afford fewer library books, what do we cut? All books by authors whose initials come in the second half of the alphabet? If the equipment fund is cut, does it make sense to buy half a sewing machine, just the keyboard of a computer, or only the circular parts of a potter's wheel?

Pressure for improved funding must therefore continue, and we must insist that development projects on the lines of the Schools Council and the MEP should persist, in some more practical form than hitherto. For any major curriculum initiative to succeed, there must be appropriate contributory factors and it is well to remember that the track record of many Schools Council projects was discouraging. All too often teams worked long hours producing useful packages and investigating interesting lines of approach, but with an impetus rather at a tangent to the main stream of classroom teacher concern. Dissemination was ineptly handled and follow-up was partial or non-existent. What was worse was the lack of continued support once the projects had done their initial work. Teachers were still grappling with the resultant problems, and particularly the problems that arose after the original curriculum materials had been produced. (For instance, the growing interest in multiculturalism and the attack on racism has meant a reappraisal even of well-respected resources and textbooks.) Worthwhile initiatives died of starvation and discouragement.

Needs, opportunities and appropriate structures can be determined, and people in high places, or off on middle-level tangents, can produce plans and reports, even standards and personnel, and yet very little can result. This is not just a British problem. To the casual visitor, nothing could seem more successful in American high schools than the library media center movement: media centers are established in most schools, are 'required' by most state authorities, and are well stocked and staffed. Yet as I showed elsewhere[1], despite a series of impressive-sounding reports and long decades of dedicated work at many levels, including a magnificent 580-page standard banner-bearing text by Ruth Ann Davies[2], it was clear that there was considerable dissatisfaction among leaders of the media center movement with the impact and use of such centers, and much 'between the lines' evidence in Ruth Ann Davies's masterwork itself that the major aspirations of most national policy documents for education were only being met in the most limited way. Even in the third edition (1979), she was still reporting 'the classroom/textbook lockstep', 'rote recall' and a lack of overall curriculum planning, from all of which sins not only her book but the earlier policy statements which formed her inspiration sought to deliver us.

For any movement to succeed in education, it must perform the difficult task of enthusing its supporters while at the same time tackling the doubts and criticisms of its detractors and the cautious misgivings of everyone else. It must 'show results' while at the same time recognising that most really important results are untestable and unquantifiable. It must deal, moreover, with the genuine practical problems faced by well-intentioned teachers trying to put its precepts into practice, on the basis that if X is more difficult to do than Y, eventually most people are going to need very good reasons indeed to continue with X.

A renewed emphasis on enquiry skills is stimulated by the developments in computer technology but does not depend upon such developments, nor is it the only response to them. Whether or not the 'new information society' as futurologists envisage it comes to pass in quite the way they suggest, we already inhabit a world in which information proliferates in a bewildering range of formats and is increasingly essential for confident success in all areas of adult life. Thus it is not only information technologists in the new sense who ask about 'the use of knowing'; indeed, not all of them by any means have recognized it as a problem. Nonetheless the earlier protagonists of enquiry did not always foresee the implications of the methodology they proposed (particularly its implications for organization, material support, professional help and, crucially, monitoring what happened). New information technology is not 'the answer' but can help us to seek out better solutions to the sometimes unanticipated difficulties that arose. At the same time it gives us a natural focus for discussion and planning. We can more confidently call for a rearrangement of priorities in both teaching and examining, an emphasis not only on 'process' as well as 'content', but what is learnt thereby, 'the content of process'. Such a stance can unite traditionalists and progressivists alike; it is no longer either-or; we cannot be other than eclectic. And the newest technologies — as I write, computers and videodiscs — link with the oldest in facilitating synthesis.

There are implications for teachers, heads of department, heads of resources, school librarians, teachers in charge of computing, head teachers, local education authorities, pre- and in-service trainers, supply services, commercial agencies, research projects, universities, the inspectorate and the DES, and finally for the information technology industry itself in all its aspects. In these pages we can only tease out some of them, but it is hoped they will prove suggestive and that others will be able to build upon them.

But the biggest single change, so far as the secondary sector is concerned, may come about by a simple decision of the various examining boards. They are re-examining their syllabuses and guidelines, their examination papers and marking schedules, as well as looking at other ways in which student achievement could be demonstrated: and they are listing and finding appropriate ways of testing the possession of, the skills of search, including the conceptualization of need and the evaluation of evidence, which some of their prescriptions already, by inference, presuppose. Such a changed emphasis has long been urged from many quarters and with different purposes: it is surely appropriate now, when so much concern is being expressed about standards and the relevance of educational systems for the future of our society, that this simple but revolutionary step was taken by those who test and grade our children. The new General Certificate in Secondary Education is a welcome step.

Within Schools

Primary Schools: The Foundations for Enquiry Competence

Let us now go back to the grass roots ('the chalk face') and see what arises when we examine the needs of schools in our new context. We begin with the first stage of compulsory schooling, where there is at present the greatest concentration on skills learning as distinct from content. At the primary stage children learn to read, write and calculate, they learn a variety of social skills and understandings, and they gain their first insights into what 'school learning' might be about. Primary children have many problems, but they are quite unsurprised by technology and unself-conscious in its use, and despite the doubts which secondary teachers sometimes express about the abilities of 12-year-olds, primary children still mastering manual and other bodily skills nonetheless cope extremely well with machinery without damaging it or them. Being at the 'concrete operations' stage, they need plenty of activity and learn by doing, but rapidly lose interest in problems that cannot be solved on the spot: thus an information delivery system that promised them 'a book with the answer in, in two weeks' time' would be little use.

Primary teachers already spend much of their time on skills development but Pat Avann's account[3] of her work developing an understanding of library and enquiry skills with primary teachers shows some of the uncertainties that need to be explained and the underlying lack of confidence many such teachers feel. Computers are (as we saw) already being used in the primary sector for mathematical work (especially with the use of LOGO where the children themselves instruct the machine) and for language-stimulating activities, often using games as a basis. We saw that programs are available (varying in quality) which can be used during projects, both for controlling the activity itself and for recording and manipulating the data produced. Some work is simple and there is plenty of scope for the teacher-produced program linked to local interests and also to other available resources; moreover the size of such resource collections is rarely so large that the average teacher cannot appraise it for suitable material in project planning. Primary teachers do, however, have problems finding time and opportunity to track down and appraise resource items new to them, particularly audiovisual and computer programs which by their nature cannot be skimmed.

Primary school needs in the context of the present chapter therefore include:

1   Guidance in the ways in which the youngest children can be introduced to computers and other information technology meaningfully, and especially ways in which the children themselves control the machine and make it give them results.
2   Guidance in how to produce simple programs which can be used with and by primary children, both in the classroom and (recreationally) in, for instance, a lunchtime library or computer games area.
3   Guidance in how to appraise and select materials, including computer programs, for use with children. The experience in 2 above would be particularly helpful here.
4   Guidance in identifying the existence of such materials: where to find catalogues and listings, where to find reviews, what to look out for in such lists and reviews, how to order, where to go to inspect items (if there are suitable services locally) etc.
5   Guidance in information skills, for instance the 'nine steps'[4]

and the integration of this understanding into the planning and oversight of projects. This might need to be broken down further: for instance, specific 'library skills' (a sub-system of information skills as a whole) as they might be presented to primary school children in relation to libraries available to them.

6 Organization of information materials. The larger the school, the more likely it is that its learning resources can be helpfully organized into central and disseminated collections. Certainly primary classrooms should be full of information materials ('surrounded by books') but children also need to learn, as soon as possible, how to interrogate and use a larger collection. There is little doubt of the value of organizing a primary school central collection on lines that match similar collections elsewhere, even if with added sub-systems such as colour-coding to help comprehension. Teachers sometimes reveal their own weaknesses here. Primary teachers who say 'Children don't understand Dewey' show they have not understood decimal classification themselves; children pick it up naturally and easily unless confused by adults. On the whole, primary children do not expect systems to make perfect sense all the time!

7 Availability of materials from elsewhere. Primary schools are normally (in this country) moderately small in size and have much smaller funds to dispense than secondaries. They benefit supremely from 'project loans' from schools library services and museum services, and would benefit by similar services being made more readily available for other media. They would also benefit by having ready access to information about what actual materials are available from such sources, and in theory there is no reason why on-line catalogues should not be provided to tell them.

8 Coordination of information and data. Teachers at all levels need all the information they can get on sources, people, places, buildings, agencies, producers, services.... Schools have sometimes produced their own classified lists, based on the knowledge and experience of their own various teachers; such lists can usefully be pooled and form the basis of local resource guides. Teachers centres (where they still exist) or LEA advisers could coordinate their collection and editing, and distribution; alternatively the schools library service could be asked to do it. Like other items in this list, such work will

only begin when teachers themselves demonstrate a con-
vincingly persistent demand.

9 Coordination of curriculum and teaching. Most primary
   schools have staff meeting discussions so that teachers are not
   working wholly independently of each other. A useful focus
   for general updating and rethinking is provided by special
   meetings to plan new activities, (for example, the introduction
   of computers or new uses for them; the introduction of a
   definite policy for information skills throughout the school;
   the working out of multicultural activities and the monitoring of resources to weed out unnecessarily offensive items)
   helping the teaching team to match the challenge of change

Much of the guidance called for in this list can be met in two
ways: by the provision of an appropriate local authority support
structure on the one hand, and of in-service courses of varying
duration on the other. The difficulty at the primary level at present is
that because of staffing constraints, individuals cannot easily be spared
during the school day, a problem which must be tackled if some
kinds of in-service courses are to be plannable. Equally, however,
some in-service training is best done on a whole-staff basis, using
'occasional' holidays when all teachers can join together in the
investigation of a particular area of concern. The goodwill of the staff
in attending any in-service programme is important to preserve and
nourish, as Secretaries of State find to their cost.

Secondary Schools: The Steps Towards Autonomy

We have not, by any means, exhausted the primary scene but at this
stage we can usefully bring our interim conclusions into the secondary
area. There is much overlap of need but we can also differentiate and
add. [I am, of course, aware that in some places the sharp distinctions
between primary and secondary are softened by an intervening
'middle school' period, so that the children may not define themselves
as 'secondary' until the age of 13 or 14. Readers will make appropriate
adjustments as they read.]

The obvious difference at the secondary stage is that so much of
the work is subject-based, with sharply decreasing opportunity for
interdisciplinary activity. This is not just an accidental decision of the
school: it is the basis of each teacher's professional identity. The
students received from the primary school are inducted into a setting

where the mastery of content becomes increasingly important and where their own growing ability to think logically and analytically can be developed. Children at the secondary stage are increasingly individual and rebellious, passing through the deeply unsettling emotions of adolescence and more sensitively aware of divisions and tensions in the society around them. By the secondary stage, there has been time for differential increments of learning and non-learning to accrue, so that for some students there is a long and demotivating history of perceived failure to contend with. Yet even with the most disruptive, it is not that they refuse to learn but what they refuse to learn that is the focus of interest to the attentive teacher. Children are still learning, even if what they are learning is counterproductive to success in the school's terms. This includes their view of themselves and what they learn from each other and from the 'hidden curriculum' of school and society.

Secondary teachers are therefore constitutionally committed to seeing each student in terms of their own subject field and its particular disciplines, and judging each teaching possibility in relation to their own ability to control potential riot. Computers are being used in secondary schools, on a modest scale, for a wide range of activities, of which probably the most popular at present (with both teachers and students) is vocationally-oriented computer studies work. Almost all secondary schools have some form of library, though not always one that is interpreted in curriculum-related terms, and various assignments make assumptions that include (as we saw) information skills, even though these may not have been made articulate in the teacher's mind. Although not all secondary school students have entered for examinations at 16+ and after, the underlying assumptions of these examinations, their syllabuses and the importance of 'covering' the content, loom largely in teachers' thinking.

Secondary school needs in the context of the present chapter therefore include:

1 Guidance in the multiple possibilities of computers and other examples of information technology in the educational work of the secondary student, and particularly those ways in which the student is actively using the machine to construct answers or to interrogate and manipulate data.

2 Guidance in the production of programs. Secondary level work may very well reach a level of complexity that makes the production of quality programs difficult and time-consuming, but teachers may benefit from being able to

understand such production, and perhaps to modify programs produced for them by others. In any case, an understanding of what is involved in program making is a valuable element in understanding computer use as a whole and also in evaluating programs produced by others.

3   Guidance in how to appraise and select materials, including computer programs, for use in curriculum-related work. Most serving teachers at present received their initial training in a world bounded by textbooks and very simple audio-visual materials, and by traditional lesson-planning assumptions. Many of those trained in more recent years were none the less taught by lecturers whose school experience was much earlier (see later comments on teacher training, page 130ff.).

4   Guidance in identifying the existence of materials (as with the primary school colleague): where to find catalogues and listings, reviews, specimen collections, and what to look out for when consulting them. If there are local collections, what they offer and how one gets access to them. (It continues to surprise me how often the existence of helpful services and collections is unknown to teachers who work only a short bus-journey away.)

5   Guidance in information skills, including the 'nine steps'[4] and the integration of this understanding into the planning of assignments. This guidance will initially focus on the use of such skills in the individual subject area of each teacher, but teachers need to be led to see the 'across the curriculum' implications and the importance of whole-school planning.[5]

6   Organization of information materials. Most secondary schools have a library and many have a wider resources organization, but an information-skills curriculum implies a much more thorough coordination of provision in order to maximize potential. Where persons with skills in resource collecting and the organization of knowledge exist within the school (typically, those schools with chartered librarians or those teachers with a recent certificate of school library studies) they should play an appropriately important part in the management planning here, in cooperation wherever possible with those colleagues who possess related skills, such as the specialist in computer studies. Because of their key position and the services they could be initiating or facilitating, all school librarians of whatever kind should produce

their own personal policy guidelines for a phased development programme, coordinating and informing.

7   Availability of materials from elsewhere. No school can be self-sufficient and the secondary school depends heavily on outside support agencies, including the schools library service, the museums service if any, film libraries and so on. Again, the time of the teacher would be significantly saved if proper information access was available to show precisely what could be obtained from where, and despite financial limitations the possibility of on-line catalogues of central services should be explored.

8   Coordination of information and data. Like their primary school colleagues, secondary teachers depend on information they glean on sources, people, places, buildings, agencies, visiting speakers, producers, services and associations. Someone should and could be pooling such information, both within the school and at area or local authority level.

9   Coordination of curriculum and teaching. Because secondary schools are so departmentally-based and subject-oriented, it is very important for there to be cross-curricular discussion of items of whole-school interest. These include overall school aims, as well as the introduction of new technology and innovative practices. As with the primary school, a recent focus will or should have been the introduction of multicultural approaches and the screening of potentially racist items. A whole-school policy towards information skills and enquiry/research methodologies has been urged in these pages, and every school needs a carefully articulated policy for its library, its information resources and its resource production facilities. A school that gets the habit of planning together stimulates interdisciplinary and cooperative thinking amongst its teaching staff.

It will be apparent that these nine points repeat, with modifications, those made for the primary sector, and I believe there will be general acceptance that any differences are mainly of emphasis — including the existence of larger collections and the specialist orientation of secondary teachers. Throughout school life, the child is growing and developing, and all schools however selective contain a wide range of personalities and present abilities.

Because of the subject concentration of secondary schools, however, there are likely to be very different perceptions of the relevance and application of information technology and research skills throughout the staff, and it may be useful to have departmental discussions, followed by a series of follow-up discussions where departments coming to similar conclusions, and then those coming to very divergent conclusions, meet to share viewpoints. From such discussions, useful evidence might be collected which could be assessed at a whole-staff meeting considering 'across the curriculum' objectives. One remembers that 'interdisciplinary team-teaching' often broke down in the past because the participants were pulled in opposite directions: loyalty to the concept and equal loyalty to the testimony of their own subject. Discussion needs to tease out such contradictions, not in order to eliminate them but to see that they are properly absorbed in a larger plan or format that allows them to be both expressed and transcended.

The School Management Team

This brings us into areas of decision which are properly those of the head and other senior members of the management hierarchy. The old days when the headteacher was absolute ruler have long gone, deriving as they did from a 'fixed' concept of education which is no longer tenable, but which left the head with a simple and disciplinary role. Today's schools run on a wide variety of management models, but all involve some measure of discussion and participative decision-making, however inadequate. In a period of constant change and upheaval, there are two factors acting in opposition to each other: on the one hand, teachers as professionals cannot be ruled by diktat but must at least passively assent to the requirements put upon them (including the very sensitive issue of how and what they should teach); on the other hand, decisions have to be made, often in circumstances in which wholehearted agreement or unanimity is impossible, and it is the role of management to shoulder the responsibility for decisions when they are complex and difficult in this way.

This is particularly relevant in view of the recognition in the previous chapter that setting up organizational structures was not, by itself, going to resolve the problems this book was addressing. Teaching styles, it is often argued, are very much a personal matter, even a personality matter, and teachers whose preference is for 'direct teaching' (instruction) are not going to move towards 'enquiry' just because they are given organizations to call on and resources to use.

Precisely so: and this is why an important element in the move towards what we might call 'research literacy' is to get it actually recognized in the curriculum, for teaching is not only a personality matter, though personality necessarily affects what any teacher does. It is a question of how particular matters can best be learnt; and the decision, in the end, on what the school is attempting to teach (with, by implication, guidance on relevant teaching approaches), rests with senior management, the headteacher, deputies, and other personnel who may be admitted to the planning team. Different teachers may still, very properly, have their own modes of operation, but are also responsible for monitoring success.

Among the many decisions facing school management teams (and especially headteachers) with the onset of information technology are the following:

1   The setting up of appropriate planning systems so that new developments in information technology can be continuously monitored by, and brought to the attention of, teaching and other staff, and implications properly and fully discussed.

2   The formulation of a school planning policy for information technology that will (a) establish a realistic platform for immediate action; and (b) allow for principled but unpredictable development as circumstances allow and require in future.

3   The reformulation of the school's policy with regard to other information resources, including the library, audiovisual materials if separate from the library, reprographic work etc, taking account of the addition of computer technology to the resources provision of the school. Staff concerned with each of these sections can be asked to produce a discussion document, separately or together, showing how service can be improved and what cooperation can develop.

These three decisions have implications for staff development and in-service training, and it will be important to see that such benefits are not restricted to one subject area or section of the staff but spread around. Not only does this offer the appearance of even-handed fairness, but it makes possible a wider spread of feedback from different subject groupings and different teaching stances. Many schools have already taken action in these two directions and have in consequence a better idea of where they may be hoping to develop further in the near future. As we saw in the section on primary schools, there are distinct advantages to be considered in setting aside a 'staff training day' when the staff as a whole can be both inducted into new learning and set to discuss its relevance for themselves and the work of the school.

We have argued that all three points above lead to a need to reconsider the way information and research skills are developed throughout the school, and therefore the next point is:

4   The reconsideration of skill development throughout the school, with special reference to the need to develop confidence in research and enquiry skills. A whole-staff discussion with preparatory reading and deliberations in departments (perhaps using Schools Council Curriculum Bulletin 9 as a basis)[6] should give the head and others the basis for a clear statement of policy. If the school library is in charge of a professional librarian who is not a member of teaching staff, it is strongly recommended that this person be invited to take part in the discussions and prepare a contributory paper.

5   As a result there may well be a need to reconsider the earlier points, particularly 2 and 3, reappraising the resourcing of the school and the organizational structure resulting. This is likely to lead to:

6   A reconsideration of recommendations likely to be urged on the local education authority as a whole and its various supporting structures, on the lines discussed in our two final chapters.

Outside the School

The Local Authority

When the Microelectronics Education Project was established in 1981, schools and local authorities had a recognized national organization with which they could collaborate in the exploration of new information technology and its educational applications. With the planned termination of MEP and its replacement by a smaller, less ambitious programme, LEAs are, perhaps usefully, thrown back on their own initiatives and most of what results will depend importantly on what they decide. Among the implications they will be discussing are:

1   *The provision of information*
    Teachers and schools (and LEA officials) have a great need for

constant updating on developments including those in IT. Although there will remain some agencies providing this at a regional or national level (which it is unnecessary for the LEA to attempt to duplicate) the LEA is an appropriate body to seek to provide from within itself a suitable organization simply for gathering and disseminating data.

2   The provision of in-service courses

The pace of change is so fast that there will always be a need for updating on IT, but there are still teachers, perhaps a majority of teachers, who have not been on any computer-related courses but who would benefit from them. In arranging for such in-service education, the LEA will naturally take into account other agencies within its domain (colleges, institutes, universities) which may have the expertise and facilities for participating in such work.

3   The development of materials

Suitable units should be established so that experimental and developmental work in the provision of software (programs) can continue, with support. Again there may be other people with whom cooperative structures can be built up in a beneficial way. Questions of ownership of copyright in any materials produced will need to be examined and answered in ways that do not discourage cooperation or enterprise.

4   The promotion of networks

Departments, units and agencies should not develop on their own without facilities for linking up with other people whose interests overlap. These networks can be both formal and informal, but if the latter, should nonetheless have some official recognition so that problems (such as over payment of minor incidental expenses) do not unnecessarily arise.

Beyond the borders of computer technology itself, there are important areas of cooperation that need examining.

5   Cooperation within in-service training

Information technology exists within a context, and in-service courses in many other specialist areas have IT dimensions (and vice versa) which will only be explored if the people in charge take an interdisciplinary overview. It is important that specialist lecturers joining a course outside their normal domain should be ready to go as listeners as well as missionaries or advertisers.

6   Cooperation within resource provision

Computer programs are only one example of software provision, and there is much to be said for a reexamination of supply services within an LEA to see if coordination can bring about economy and efficiency. Most LEAs nowadays (with significant exceptions in some big cities) maintain a schools library service, whose dissemination skills are well suited to the provision of all kinds of information materials, printed, audiovisual or electronic. There seems no reason to multiply such lending services unnecessarily.

However there is every reason to believe that new information technology could very significantly improve the quality of service offered by the SLS. Although costs are at present still high, planning should begin now towards eventual provision of computerised catalogue services. Such catalogues should aim at maximizing flexibility and cross-referencing. In larger authorities, it might already be possible to provide computer-produced microfiche copies of the total SLS catalogue, very cheaply, and regularly updated; online service using a modem and an ordinary telephone line should soon be equally possible.

7   Cooperation between advisory staff

There is a tendency within LEA advisory services for interests to be compartmentalized, sometimes on a somewhat accidental basis depending on the interests and background of each incumbent and the needs of the department at that particular time. Advisers generally take pains to be as flexible and as cooperative as they can, and to keep up with developments in other fields. However the traditional linking of computers with mathematics and (say) libraries with English does not lend itself easily to the kinds of cross-curricular thinking we have identified as being necessary. In the crowded working year of the local adviser, there ought to be times when broader thinking is encouraged and cooperative brainstorming sessions enjoined.

8   Cooperation across local authority services

Within most local authorities there is an administrative divide between the education services, under the education committee, and the library services, typically (and perversely) linked with swimming pools and parks under the leisure services committee. Not only does this lead to difficulties of contact and sometimes of easy cooperation between education and library staff, it almost invariably means that the schools library service chief is not present at meetings of education advisers nor accorded similar status in terms of respect and committee access. Thus a valuable input is missing from many discussions and the library service is less easily able to make appropriate and timely provision. Absurd situations arise, such as a famous conference occasion when a chief education officer said, 'Unfortunately we have no-one available who is an expert on information' — and the head of schools library service was sitting three chairs away.

9   Policy statements

With the cooperation of all services, the LEA would be able, as some have done already, to produce detailed policy statements for the various aspects of information provision within the authority. We have already indicated our conviction that there are important links between them, but it is striking how few LEAs have produced policy documents for forward planning on computer technology, on the role of school libraries and of the schools library services, and on the impact on educational need of the 'new information society' which we already inhabit and which futurologists predict the growth of. Authorities who do not wish to be over-rash might helpfully concentrate on the first two: it must now be possible for an authority to come to a considered view on the present and immediate future plans it has for utilizing and promoting computer technology; and libraries have been around long enough, one might respectfully suggest, for LEAs to feel confident about the kind of policy statement urged upon them by LISC.[7]

10   Other professionals and in-service training

Local authorities should also note the existence of a number of professions in and around education as well as teachers themselves. Present conditions of service make it remarkably difficult for many such professionals to gain additional professional understanding beyond the minimum demands of their present post (there is, for instance, no provision for secondment or study leave), and no salary enhancement is given to professionals on the administrative and professional grades who gain additional qualifications enabling them to do their job with more understanding.

One example, very relevant to our exploration of the demands of an 'information-rich society' is the school librarian or member of the schools library service. Many reports[8,9] have drawn attention to the importance of 'double qualification', in librarianship and education, for such people; yet those few who have so far struggled to obtain such qualifications get no encouragement, no reward and no recognition. It would be helpful if NALGO and the local authorities sat down to tackle this problem, which at present discourages initiative and leads to the kinds of 'tunnel vision' we have been deploring. One suspects that other professionals in and around education are in a similar position.

Professional Training

Much used to be claimed for, and expected of, teacher training institutions. They were the experts: they set the standards: they did the research: on the basis of their professional wisdom, they set new entrants to the profession up with the methodologies they should employ, the insights they would need, the concepts they should hold. 'The methods now being taught in teacher training institutions' is a phrase redolent with overtones of innovation, expertise, and frontiersmanship. In contrast, the old hands in school staff rooms deliberately and dedicatedly set out to break new teachers' confidence in their mentors and to show that what was most needed was a few years' practical experience 'on the job', after which the 'new-fangled nonsense' supposedly being purveyed by the colleges and institutes would be knocked out of them.

Three decades in and around such teacher-training institutions, and in and around schools, convinces me that both views are greatly exaggerated. Much dedicated study is done, in the colleges, schools and institutes of education, of what is actually happening in schools and what research is telling us that can help. The observant spectator sees what the player is too busy to note, and the teacher whose experience is at best limited to two or three schools (especially if all these schools were in the same area or local authority) should be cautious about generalizing from such a limited sample. But lecturers in education tend to bring with them the insights and enthusiasms which were current at the time of their translation, and ever after are dependent for their information and stimulus on the innovative schools where the 'action' is; and the focal points for such innovation tend to move around, as the patterns of change alter and new factors emerge to put yesterday's centres of excellence well out of the top twenty.

Thus teacher-training institutions tend to present a fairly conservative picture, and the main reason why they are sometimes charged with 'new-fangled innovation' is that they at least suggest alternative possibilities, the existence of which the closed mind of the hardened staff room traditionalist will not accept. They may still, because they have the opportunity and (importantly) access to the literature of what other teachers elsewhere are reporting, have a considerable expertise to offer the new trainee, but only in partnership with the schools within which this trainee is gaining the important practical part of professional induction.

Yet the crucial point goes beyond this. It is that in the initial course there are severe limitations to what can be taught, because the neophyte teacher is spending much of the time gaining confidence and understanding, learning through personal experience what the profession and craft of teaching involves and making personal adjustments to its demands. For this the accumulated traditional wisdom of the profession is very important, and new teachers are generally (by common observation) less innovative, less ready to make daring experiments, than their rather more mature colleagues with (say) five or six years of successful experience. All that initial training can do (and it is an important contribution) is give a general overall picture of the profession, its main philosophies and tendencies, an insight into the varied backgrounds of schoolchildren and what so far is known about the underlying reasons for individual differences in achievement, and a methodology by which the new teacher can analyze the task ahead and the successes and failures that will follow. This will be even more true if the present trend towards one-year postgraduate training, rather than three-year BEd training, continues. A year of thirty-six class-contact weeks is very short for all that needs to be said and done as a starter.

If the influence of teacher-training institutions depended on the success of initial courses, it would be very limited indeed, because the vast majority of teachers in post have already been trained (in whatever 'methods' were current at that time) and will presumably be untouched by what happens in other people's initial courses. The major claim to influence of (for instance) the university schools and institutes of education lies in their post-experience courses and in the research they undertake, especially that research which is undertaken in close symbiosis with schools at the chalk face.

This preamble was to answer in advance those who may have extravagant expectations from changes in initial courses of teacher-training. One hopes that today all such courses will include significant sections on the uses of new information technology: and that this work will not be restricted either to mathematical implications (important though these are) or to instructional programs. One hopes that the challenges presented by the pace of social, technological and professional change will be kept prominently in view, and that the importance of the skills learnt during process will be emphasized (including information and research skills of the kind we have discussed). It would also be excellent, and astonishingly untypical, if the existence of the library as a major teaching tool for use in curriculum-related activities was emphasized and explored. Generally speaking, where libraries are mentioned in initial courses, it is in optional modules for those particularly concerned with how they are organized. Nearly fifty years after the formation of the School Library Association, and nearly a hundred years since the Cross Commission came out in favour of libraries in elementary schools, one would have hoped that curricular uses of such entities would have been noted by the experts; at a time when the ability to access and assess information for oneself has become so important, it is a vital part of the new teacher's professional understanding.

In earlier chapters the phrase 'tunnel vision' was introduced, and this is the point to remind all institutions concerned with professional training that there are related professions whose members would benefit from the insight gained from their courses. The experiment of the ILEA 'Media Resources Officer' showed the value of having a resources consultant in schools, able to advise on resources production and where appropriate to produce such materials on request — with expertise that was not only audiovisual and reprographic but educational, based on a very strong education component within the training as well as, frequently, educational knowledge possessed by the MRO before training. Similarly, there are at present between five and six hundred chartered librarians working in school libraries, and more working in sixth form colleges, further education colleges and schools library services, for whom the possession of a solid background of education understanding would be a personally valued contribution to their professional work.

In the 'new information society' the information professionals should be encouraged to work alongside teachers and with as much understanding as possible. Various reports, including the Bullock Report *A Language for life*[9] and the LISC document, *School Libraries: The Foundations of the Curriculum*[10], have either called for or endorsed 'double qualification' for school librarians, in both education and librarianship, and the two associations responsible for school librarians[11] have given qualified approval in principle. It remains astonishingly difficult for people seen as being 'in' one profession to gain introductory (let alone professional) understanding of another, and both teacher training institutions and departments of library and information studies should be encouraged to try harder, and to press local and national authorities harder, in this respect. Other countries, notably the USA, Canada and Australia, have a much more flexible and 'user-friendly' system for advanced education than our own.

In cooperation with local authorities, professional schools should also be examining what courses might be offered to computer experts anxious to work in the education field, and to audiovisual producers similarly placed. In-service courses for teachers or other professionals might well make a point of seeing that related professions are invited to send students to the courses for mutual enrichment; I have personally found the co-presence of teachers, media resource officers and librarians in the same short course classroom immensely stimulating in the insights that resulted.

National Initiatives

There have been expressions of concern in the teaching profession that big government should not intrude improperly into areas of professional concern, by which is normally meant the curriculum. This book is not the place for a detailed discussion, but my view broadly is that any governmental action should be concerned with arriving at a non-partisan consensus on essential elements to be included in curricula. It is within governmental propriety, for instance, to conclude that schools should give proper emphasis to technology, and correct to state that many schools have tended to undervalue engineering as an appropriate student aspiration. It is proper for government to ask schools to make every effort to work towards racial harmony, in line with the intentions behind Acts of Parliament. It is not proper for government, on its own, to lay down proportions of time to be spent on this and that, and it is quite improper of government to seek to put pressure on schools not to discuss matters of adult controversy, so long as these matters are properly addressed (and whether they are or not is primarily a professional, not a political, decision).

Thus it was excellent of government to set up the Microelectronics Education Project, as an initiative to encourage teachers to make fuller use of, and give closer attention to, the new information technology. Her Majesty's Inspectorate, equally, has the right and duty to advise both government and the profession on matters of concern to them, and we have the right to call some areas of interest to their attention. In setting up new examinations and examining boards, and bodies such as the School Curriculum

Development Council, the Secondary Examinations Council, and the Council for Educational Technology, the government 'intervened' in education without necessarily improperly biassing practice (whether or not one necessarily agrees with the divisions between such bodies or likes the individuals appointed to their boards).

This preamble was necessary because some enthusiastic prophets have seen the future of new technology as offering a splendid chance for government to establish new patterns of automated provision, rather in the way that Sweden established nationwide mathematics teaching through resource packs. Any such notions would, as we saw in earlier chapters, overlook major areas of educational concern, and there is reason to believe that the vision is receding, but it may well be lingering in the folk-memory of the more alert members of the profession — and big business may yet seek to maximize some otherwise unnoticed potential by going for the big one.

The shopping-list of recommendations emerging from the argument of this book, so far as any agency of central government is concerned, would surely include the following:

1 To take the lead in stimulating thorough-going debate on the implications of new and imminent information technology, in realistic but imaginative terms, within and throughout all levels of the teaching profession and the professions which serve it, as well as with employers associations and special interest groups.

2 To take the lead in initiating discussion on the implications, not just of new technology, but of our current information-rich society, and the need for schoolchildren to be thoroughly prepared for adult life within it. This would include discussion with all groups concerned with information provision.

3 To take a national initiative in the field of staff training, similar to the MEP programme but emphasizing all forms of information and publication. This would mean not only teachers but librarians, media specialists, and other professionals. We indicated earlier (page 129) that the present system of higher education, secondment and in-service training was inhospitable to those lateral thinkers who wished to broaden their base of professional understanding.

4 To recognize that new developments in education cannot proceed on a basis of decreasing funding, whatever the situation of 'falling rolls'. It is not a question of improving education by 'throwing money at it', but recognizing the impor-

ance of making use of facilities and technologies which are costly, though not extravagantly so. Although every effort should be made to divert funds from 'less necessary' activities, the depredations of recent years make the scope for savings from such diversions fairly marginal. (Fortunately, the cost of computers is dropping in real terms, though not necessarily the cost of the most effective level of computers — the cheaper micros may not be the best answers. The cost of other necessary technologies, such as books, is at best stable or slightly rising.)

5   To produce challenge funds for local authorities ready to make initiatives and produce sensible development plans for all forms of information provision, including computer services, libraries and other agencies, preferably on an integrated pattern.

6   In the light of new developments, and the recognition of the importance of information handling skills, to produce new guidelines for computer/audiovisual/library provision in schools, including space provision, guidelines for stock and technology, and maintenance. At the same time, to undertake regular surveys of such provision and publish the results.

7   To establish a coordinating body so that all developments in the field of information can be properly monitored and discussed by representatives from organizations concerned.

8   To strengthen the expertise available within and to HMI team, by including experienced librarians, educational technologists and others, with appropriate terms of reference.

Government and Industry

Service to education forms only a small part of the computer industry, and it is therefore important both for the industry itself and for the rest of us if there is some measure of agreement on what the most advantageous contribution from that small part could be. Up to the time of writing, the record of the Department of Education and Science here has been undistinguished; and the biggest single contribution to the current state of play in computers in British education was the initiative of the Department of Trade and Industry, whose negotiations with Acorn and the BBC led to the production of a standard microcomputer of acceptable quality and with a reasonably structured form of BASIC which could be afforded by many schools and for which it made sense to produce a range of appropriate software — the programs which schools could purchase and use. Some I think would argue that this initiative was in the short run more influential than anything undertaken by the Microelectronics Education Project itself — and MEP were not involved in the decision.

It seems reasonably clear that we need:

1 Agreement on acceptable standard models at different levels of performance and cost which schools and colleges could aim for, which could then be economically mass produced at affordable prices, and for which software can be written with confidence that a market will be available for it.

2 Agreement if possible on important areas of concentration for software producers — without prejudice to the speculative creativity of the mavericks. Programs giving a framework for project-type activity should be included among the priorities.

3 Detailed discussions, bringing in the telecommunications industry, on the provision of suitably priced network facilities, to take advantage of the wider facilities which the new information technology offers.

4 Discussions with the manufacturers of videodiscs, to examine the possibilities of a standard format affordable throughout the education system over the longer term, so that the technology's implications for data storage and interactive facilities can be creatively but also responsibly explored.

5 Initiation of discussions between educational book publishers and the computer and videodisc industry, to investigate the possibilities of tie-ups and cooperative provision. The broadcasting authorities and the private agencies around them should also be part of these consultations. (One envisages the possibility of a prestige television series, both popular and educational, for which schools and colleges would buy or lease interactive videodisc and computer program software, together with accompanying print material, and perhaps 'the BBC book of the series'. The Domesday Project may turn out to be the pilot for something much more elaborate; as well as the official material, smaller agencies might well produce their own supplementary software with a distinctive contribution.)

Professional Associations

Although one accepts that professional associations will necessarily be primarily concerned with defending the boundaries of their concern and the immediately perceived interests of their members, one would hope they might see the importance of interprofessional discussions, bearing in mind the fact that a rapidly changing society may see a blurring of distinctions and a shifting of boundaries. At the very least:

1 *Discussions between professional associations and unions* in the related fields of education, computer technology, educational technology, librarianship and information science, and similar areas, to discuss collaborative action and matters of common concern.

2 *Discussions between professional associations and institutions offering professional education*, with a view to providing modular and other courses (both in college and through distance teaching) at initial training and post-experience level, for those whose terms and conditions of service make fulltime attendance difficult; and to consider what might reasonably and helpfully be offered to professionals in other related disciplines who might need or profit from additional expertise.

3 *Discussions between professional associations* concerning initiatives which might be proposed to local authorities and national government, on matters of joint concern.

4 *Discussions within professional associations*, to determine whether their main policies and structures for decision-making make appropriate allowance for smaller groups within these associations who might be moving in a cross-disciplinary fashion or need special dispensation or provision. (To give one example: the Library Association's programme for the achievement of full professional accreditation currently fits well with the needs and circumstances of large library systems, but fails to meet the needs of those in small libraries or, like school librarians, on their own. It also makes considerable difficulties for those whose work includes, but does not consist entirely of, duties defined as 'librarianship'. I leave to my readers the articulation of the parallels I believe exist in other professions.)

Look Out For the Future

There is a limit to the patience of readers, and I am happy to leave the preceding sections of this chapter as examples to be considered with appropriate scepticism. Although I believe they arise out of the discussion of this book, they are necessarily partial and to some extent personal, although the perceptive reader who follows up the references given for earlier chapters will recognize recommendations reworked from them, often into a more interdisciplinary context.

Chapter 1 began by uneasily probing a persuasively confident assertion about the future of education, and some readers will have wondered whether the succeeding chapters were not unnecessarily cautious. It is always hard to maintain the appropriate balance between confident expectation and sceptical analysis, but both are necessary if we are to meet the challenges ahead intelligently and humanistically. Throughout the text, I have found myself deliberately repressing the more outspoken assertions of educators whose thoughts have influenced me, in case they overbalanced the discussion. Yet it is impossible leave them out entirely: the electrifying statement in the Faure Report, for instance:

> . . . for the first time in history, education is now engaged in preparing men for a type of society which does not yet exist. [12]

(What a pity it did not add 'and women', or simply refer to 'people'!)

G.B. Morris[13] surveyed the literature of futurology, identified what he called 'an observed educational lag' in coming to terms with change, and noted, 'The major priority in the future will be "how" the student learns rather than "what" he learns', adding that 'preparing individuals with "survival skills" will be a future task for educators'. Case and Parsons[14] put it this way:

> Adaptation to such a fast changing culture requires not facts and finding, but procedures and process, not organisational data but organisational skills, not storage but processing.

Norman Longworth[15] reflected that:

> As we move into the information society, what post-industrial children learn at school has a useful life of less than half a generation and much of it is obsolescent as it is taught.

Technology could liberate or enslave, but:

... it does require some little imagination to realize what the effects might be of *not* educating all children to sort out the differences between essential and non-essential information, raw fact, prejudice, half-truth and untruth so that they know when they are being manipulated. (his emphasis)

Arthur Lewis[16] said:

We cannot teach children all they will need to know to solve the problems of the next century, but ... 1. We can help students develop skills of reading, writing and computing ... [but] information alone is not enough to solve problems. The ability to comprehend that information — to analyze it, synthesize it, and apply it in a value-oriented way — is also necessary. 2. We can encourage students to assume responsibility for their own learning — to become self-directed, lifelong learners.

Such analyses make rather more impact, by the measured concern for values implicit in them, than breathless reporting of the marvellous future of computer-assisted instruction heralded by James Martin: 'To prepare such programs there has grown up an industry as large as Hollywood and just as professional'![17] (Question for students: Define 'professional' in this sentence, and comment.)

Those of us who approach future education with an enthusiasm balanced by unease do so first because we recognize that what happens in any educational process is almost always more complicated than it seems, and second because, in the last analysis, any kind of learning points students towards a world that, though possibly manageable, is difficult. Back in 1938 John Dewey reminded us of a point many programmers would do well to pin to their walls:

Perhaps the greatest of all pedagogical fallacies is the notion that a person learns only the particular thing he is studying at the time. Collateral learning in the way of formation of enduring attitudes, of likes and dislikes, may be and often is much more important than the spelling lesson or lesson in geography that is learned. For these attitudes are what fundamentally count in the future. The most important attitude that can be formed is that of the desire to go on learning.[18]

Herman Niebuhr Jr. observed, in the context of an article noting the 'paradigm shift' towards intentional and self-directed learning:

... freedom and choice are burdens. Unless the individual is given the tools to exploit such opportunities, the burden may become onerous.[19]

And W.R. Niblett[20], reflecting from his long experience on 'the time of doubt' in which we now live, commented:

In the age we live in many people find it difficult to locate sources of meaning which matter. If the education they are given by-passes the problem, that education is, I suggest, insufficient in its sense of responsibility.... To be awake to what novelists and poets ... have been saying in notes or words is on occasion to be shown where meaning lies. But shown, not instructed; it is a mistake anyway to suppose that knowledge is restricted to what can be talked about.

He went on:

Learning of the kind I am talking about is existential learning; it cannot, that is, be added to by memorization or 'hard work' alone. More self-involvement is required, more 'depth and darkness'.

It is in such contexts that discussion of the role of computer technology and other information systems needs to take place. Equally in question are the roles of other styles of teaching, whether supposedly 'traditional' or 'progressivist'. The context has changed the meaning and application of these terms, as well as the tasks and responsibilities to which we address them. As professionals we do not discard all we know because of the emergence of a new machine, but we reexamine what we need to know. And because that machine, and other forces, are entering a society which is itself in headlong change, we ask what our students need to know.

One answer is that they need to know how to know, how to deal with the sources of knowing, how to separate the plausible from the meaningful, and how to create from what they find the new meaning they must construct: the 'use of knowing'. These pages have sought to analyze this process a little from the testimony and witness of people from many places and disciplines.

Notes

1. BESWICK, N.W. (1983) 'The controversial school library: A critical re-assessment and proposed new strategy', *Education Libraries Bulletin*, 26, 2,

spring, pp. 1–15.

2. DAVIES, R.A. (1979) *The School Library Media Program: Instructional Force for Excellence*, Bowker.

3. AVANN, P. (1984) 'Information skills in primary schools', *Education Libraries Bulletin*, 27, 1, spring, pp. 1–14.

4. MARLAND, M. (Ed.). (1981) *Information skills in the Secondary Curriculum*, London, Methuen International (Schools Council Curriculum Bulletin 9).

5. IRVING, A. (1985) *Study and Information Skills Across the Curriculum*, London, Heinemann Educational Books.

6. MARLAND, M. (Ed.) (1981) *op. cit.*

7. For guidance, see IRVING, A. (1985) *op. cit.*

8. Office of Arts and Libraries, Library and Information Services Council (1984) *School Libraries: The Foundations of the Curriculum*, Report of the Working Party on School Library Services, London, HMSO, p. 25.

9. Department of Education and Science. (1975) *A Language for Life* (The Bullock Report), London, HMSO, p. 305.

10. Office of Arts and Libraries,(1984) *op. cit.* p. 12.

11. The Library Association and the School Library Association.

12. International Commission on the Development of Education (1972). *Learning To Be: The World of Education Today and Tomorrow* . (The Faure Report), Paris/London, UNESCO/Harrap.

13. MORRIS, G.B. (1982) 'A conceptualization of education in the future', *Canadian Journal of Education* 7, 2, pp. 16–33.

14. CASE, R. and PARSONS, R. (1978) 'An educational imperative for the future', *Education Tomorrow*, pp. 4–5.

15. LONGWORTH, N. (1981) 'We're moving into the information society. What shall we teach the children?', *Computer Education*. June, pp. 17–19.

16. LEWIS, A.J. (1983) 'Education for the 21st century', *Educational Leadership*, 41, 1, September, pp. 9–10.

17. MARTIN, J. (1978) *The Wired Society*, London, Prentice-Hall, p. 9.

18. DEWEY, J. (1938) *Experience and Education*, London, Collier-Macmillan, chapter 3.

19. NIEBUHR, H. Jr. (1981) 'Teaching and learning in the eighties: The paradigm shifts', *Phi Delta Kappan*, 62, 5, January, pp. 367–8.

20. NIBLETT, W.R. (1983) 'Where we are now', *Studies in Higher Education*, 8, 2, pp. 105–110.

Index